Handlin, Oscar, 1915-
    Chance or destiny; turning points in
American history.   Boston, Little, Brown
[1955]
    220 p.   22cm.

75.9
35

1. U.S.--   History--Philosophy.
I. Title.

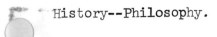

BY OSCAR HANDLIN

BOSTON'S IMMIGRANTS, 1790 – 1865
(J. H. Dunning Prize, 1941)

COMMONWEALTH: A Study of the Role of
Government in the American Economy

THIS WAS AMERICA

THE UPROOTED
(Pulitzer Prize in History, 1952)

AMERICAN PEOPLE IN THE TWENTIETH CENTURY

ADVENTURE IN FREEDOM

CHANCE OR DESTINY:
Turning Points in American History

Edited by Oscar Handlin

HARVARD GUIDE TO AMERICAN HISTORY

THE LIBRARY OF AMERICAN BIOGRAPHY

Chance or Destiny

TURNING POINTS IN
AMERICAN HISTORY

Chance or Destiny

TURNING POINTS IN
AMERICAN HISTORY

by
OSCAR HANDLIN

An Atlantic Monthly Press Book

Little, Brown and Company · Boston · Toronto

ATLANTIC—LITTLE, BROWN BOOKS
ARE PUBLISHED BY
LITTLE, BROWN AND COMPANY
IN ASSOCIATION WITH
THE ATLANTIC MONTHLY PRESS

Published simultaneously in Canada
by Little, Brown & Company (Canada) Limited

PRINTED IN THE UNITED STATES OF AMERICA

FOR RUTH

Contents

Chance or Destiny

TURNING POINTS IN AMERICAN HISTORY

Prologue

HERE are eight stories and a problem.

The stories deal with men and women, with the clash of historic forces, with the effect of accident. They examine the motives that lead to action; and they describe the passions that action produces. They have the effect of drama, with overtones of tragedy, and with flashes of comedy. In that sense these tales are interesting.

Furthermore, these stories are important. From the incidents that form the substance of this book, great results followed. The people of thirteen British colonies became a nation. The United States spread from a narrow line of settlement along the Atlantic across the continent to the Pacific. From a weak band of states, it became a great power, disposing enormous might throughout the world.

The means that effected the transformation were diplomacy and war. The conduct of both international negotiations and military operations involves extensive planning and the minute calculation of detail. Yet in all these stories, chance also played a role; and at some decisive turning point gave an unexpected twist to historical development.

Pondering the degree to which accident overturned the schemes of wise men, Prince Bismarck once concluded there was a special providence for drunkards, fools, and the United States. And indeed from the point of view of the experienced statesman or the professional soldier there was much to be said for the argument that America had survived and grown strong by a miraculous streak of luck that, at one turning point after another, directed fortune its way.

But that raises a serious question as to the nature of such turning points and their place in history. That is the problem to which the stories point.

CHAPTER ONE

Independence at Yorktown

IT takes an effort of the imagination to look back over the long distance we have come on the way to being a great power. We make our influence felt in the distant corners of the earth; and every act of politics today must take account of American will and interest. It is difficult now to recall that the road to the present was not straight or easy — that it led often by decisive turnings at which our fate was subject to the accidents of chance, to the whims of forgotten foreign statesmen, and to the firmness of certain Americans.

It is well, therefore, to remember how we, a new nation, came into being. Rebellion, war, and diplomacy were the means. But in our success were involved the miscalculations of men, the chances of casual encounters, and even the winds of the undependable weather.

The young Americans who dared aspire toward independence in 1776 lacked resources and experience and authority; they faced a powerful empire and a vigorous and resolute king. Although defiance was already a habit with them, it was a hazardous course that the members of the Continental Congress took when they determined to cut the ties that bound them to Britain.

In the next two years, they had frequent occasion to wonder at their own foolhardiness. They had staved off the first attempts at reconquest. But they had not been able to clear the English away from their coasts. And the uncertain operations of the state and central governments generated no confidence in their permanence or stability.

As the volunteer armies melted away with the fading of the first flush of enthusiasm, as the currency depreciated toward nothingness and the tax yield fell off, increasingly the only hope for success seemed the intervention of some powerful outsider. It was for this reason that American thoughts drifted often to France, where Benjamin Franklin labored to convince the government of Louis XVI that it had a stake in the struggle.

Whether France would intercede or not would be largely the decision of an aristocratic minister of state. Charles Gravier, Comte de Vergennes, had seen long service under the French crown. Born of a branch of the nobility that had distinguished itself in government, he had spent his whole active life in diplomacy, moving from one embassy to another — from Frankfort to Munich, Stockholm, and Constantinople. In 1774 he became Minister of Foreign Affairs for Louis XVI, determined to regain the ground France had lost in the disastrous succession of eighteenth-century wars.

In the polished salons of Versailles the aging courtier would take a step heavy with consequences for the New World. For Vergennes the American Revolution was a lucky chance, an opportunity for retaliation against the overconfident British, now the possessors of so many prized colonies once French. Through spies in England and agents in America he had watched discontent ripple through the seaports and back country from Massachusetts to the Carolinas, and shrewdly hoped to chart his own way through these unpredictable currents. He had cautiously advanced aid to the colonies, encouraging them to keep a disturbing sore alive in the side of his British enemy. But he remained formally a neutral until 1778.

The Battle of Saratoga the year before had given him a basis for belief that the rebels might actually gain their independence. He did not dare hope that France could win back her old empire; but judicious assistance to the Americans would weaken George III and would attach the new nation in friendship and alliance to Louis XVI. In the early spring he extended formal recognition to the new state and entered into a formal alliance with it. "No event was ever received with more heartfelt joy," wrote Washington, out of the depths of relief and renewed confidence that the news had brought.

In the alignment of powers against Britain that now took shape, the French played a critical role. Along with themselves, they drew Spain actively into the war. The Netherlands were persuaded to maintain a benevolent neutrality toward the United States until 1780, when they too became belligerents. In the north, Russia and Sweden were encouraged in "armed neutrality," almost as advantageous to the Americans as open intervention.

Now that France was openly at war with Britain, Vergennes was realist enough to know the magnitude of the task ahead. Not the man to underestimate the power of his opponent, he could envisage all the risks of defeat and was determined to avoid excessive commitments. Cautiously he maneuvered to retain freedom of action, wary, yet alert to every opportunity.

As the indecisive years went by, Vergennes's caution was justified. The pendulum of fortune swung from one side to the other; and the humiliating defeat that would bring the obdurate George III to terms was as remote as ever. An American army was in existence, and French forces had been of some assistance. But the British held the principal Atlantic cities and there was not much hope of immediately dislodging them.

Furthermore, Vergennes had paid a heavy price for Spanish assistance. The conservative court in Madrid had shied from the idea of encouraging revolutionaries; and only the promise that Gibraltar would be his reward had overcome the caution of the proud Florida-blanca, principal minister of the Spanish king. There was not, however, the least likelihood that the British would agree to a peace by which they would lose the great fortress that was the key to the western Mediterranean. To compel her to yield to such terms would prolong the war indefinitely.

Early in 1781, Vergennes therefore imagined that the time had come to end the fighting and to consolidate the gains already made. It was almost six years since the shots fired at Concord, three since the French had become belligerents. The long struggle was bleeding the treasury dry, and Louis XVI was in no position to support an indefinite drain on his purse. Much better to cut the conflict short and to realize limited gains than to hazard all in further combat.

Vergennes's plan was simple and in accord with the accepted diplomacy of the eighteenth century. The purpose of war was not the unconditional surrender or the total destruction of the enemy, but a moderate improvement of strategic position and whatever accessions of territory were not too expensive. On the battlefields of Europe the great powers were all the time trading corners of the continent. This war's foe might be the friend of the next; and unrestrained ambition was not only indecent but might provoke the united hostility of all the states committed to keeping power in balance.

The French minister's reasoning was therefore almost classic in its logic. Let peace be on the basis of the status quo. Let all the struggling powers retain what they then possessed. That would put a halt to further unprofitable expenditures in men and money and at the same time stabilize the advantages already attained.

There seemed every prospect that the war would draw to a close on some such terms as these, subject, of course, to the usual diplomatic haggling over details. This would make not a perfect but a feasible peace, Vergennes reasoned. True, Great Britain would retain New York, Savannah, and the seaports in between, and the United States would lack a proven outlet to the sea except at Boston. But on the other hand the new nation would have its independence recognized; and it would hold a substantial stretch of territory — more, indeed, than the present needs of its population required. True, also, Spain would not retake Gibraltar; but it would gain both banks of the Mississippi and the whole coast of the Gulf of Mexico. France would weaken England and strengthen its alliance with both the United States and Spain. Yet the terms were not so ruinous as to push Great Britain into unyielding resistance.

Vergennes, it happened, was somewhat reticent about bringing into the open proposals that were "lacking in delicacy," since they were far short of the expectations of his allies. It was usual in such situations to spare the sensibilities of all involved; there was no embarrassment if the initial suggestion came from neutral mediators. In this case, the Emperor of Austria and the Empress of Russia were available, and, indeed, in due course they advanced the proposal for peace which had been spelled out for them by Vergennes. All was in proper form, and rationally there seemed no reason why the terms might not be accepted when they were presented in May, 1781.

Rationally! On some questions, however, the Americans refused to be altogether rational. Strangers to diplomacy, they were not disposed to compromise. The Continental Congress had already dispatched a plenipotentiary to keep them informed of the situation and to treat with the powers concerned should peace become possible. It was fortunate that the choice for that role was John Adams, a man not given to compromise of principle or interest.

As a negotiator, Adams had the country lawyer's zeal for the welfare of his client. His brusque manner, his self-righteousness, and his scarcely concealed reflections upon other men's virtue often offended those with whom he dealt. As he moved between Versailles and The Hague, his Yankee suspicions of the titled foreigners hardened into a resolve not to let himself be outbargained. Above all, however, he burned with a fierce loyalty to the ideals of the Revolution; even then he was composing the ponderous *Defence of the Constitutions of Government of the United*

States. He would accept no such compromise of those ideals as the mediation proposal involved.

Yet before the superior force of his French ally, what weight did Adams's objections have? And Franklin, the resident minister in Paris, was older, more temperate, and familiar with European state-craft. His mind absorbed the realities of the situation, and the bird-in-hand argument impressed him. He was likely to fall in with the mediation idea.

Vergennes held all the cards. If Adams was unyield-ing, Congress could be persuaded to find another envoy. Without French aid, the Americans would be in a poor way indeed. Yet, what would the nation have been had its boundaries been drawn within the limits of Vergennes's terms? A poor, provincial territory, lacking access to the sea, meager in resources, and hemmed in by powerful unfriendly neighbors on the north, west, and south. Independence would have been in name only; the reality would have remained dependence.

For the moment, George III spared the Americans the necessity of accepting that outcome. The head-strong monarch was enraged by the very suggestion of foreign mediation in a domestic quarrel with his colonies. "I certainly, till drove to the wall, will do what I can to save the empire," he still insisted. His intransigence, now, made further negotiation futile.

But Vergennes could wait. The logic of events would

make London more tractable, and peace would take the form he had sketched.

At this critical juncture only some dramatic and altogether unattended news from overseas could have altered the complexion of those events.

The news came from Yorktown.

The early months of 1781 found American military fortunes at their lowest ebb. The Continental treasury was empty, the currency was worthless, supplies were low, and the states no longer bothered to honor requisitions. The army had all but disappeared. As enlistments expired, men drifted back to their farms, their patriotic ardor having waned through the years of dreary fighting. In the depth of winter the flare of mutiny in the Pennsylvania line had brought into the open the resentment of soldiers who found it hard to keep faith alive while they were unpaid, ill-clothed, and often hungry.

In 1781 two clumps of military strength remained. At Newport was a superb French force of 5000 men under General de Rochambeau. They had come the summer before, well equipped and bountifully supplied. But they had thus far done little other than to open the eyes of provincial New Englanders and their daughters to the potentialities of a polite society.

Near West Point, Washington himself directed the American army of scarcely 3500 men. The Virginian had aged markedly since the spring day six years earlier when he had assumed command of the Continental troops in Cambridge. Indeed, he had had a weary time of it, struggling to keep alive the dreams of honor and glory while the nagging details of administration crowded in upon him. Often his thoughts drifted to his Mount Vernon home from which he had been so long absent, while he composed labored letters to Congress explaining the necessities of his situation.

Thus far, failures were as conspicuous as success; and at the opening of the year 1781, Washington was on the verge of despair. The mutiny was a shock, and the prospects for the months ahead gloomy. A man of few intimate friendships, the general grew nervous and irritable. Worried over a near defeat in the South in March, he was driven unfairly to blame Rochambeau in letters that almost caused a break with the French.

The spring passed without a rift in the clouds of anxiety. In May, Washington saw no prospect of a glorious offensive. To his journal he confided the fear that he would be trapped again in a "bewildered and gloomy defensive" campaign.

With the French, he was faced at this time by two English armies, each larger than his own. Comfortably established in New York City was Sir Henry Clinton in command of at least 14,500 well-equipped men who were being continually reinforced from home. In the South, Lord Charles Cornwallis had gathered his 5000 veterans at Yorktown, which he was fortifying as a base for further operations.

Washington was not overdisturbed at the danger from these forces. Clinton, the ranking British commander, was neither decisive nor vigorous. He had shown a preference for resting in New York over the monotonous work of pursuing bands of Continentals through the countryside. Thus far he had displayed neither the ability nor the will to stamp out the rebellion.

But it was altogether another matter to contrive Clinton's defeat. The Americans could hold on in indefinite stalemate. But they could hardly be expected to destroy forces so superior to their own. And that, of course, had been Vergennes's reckoning, as he waited that summer for the hints of peace which he had planted to take root.

Washington yearned for victory. The thought of remaining on the defensive revolted him. He therefore set about planning Clinton's destruction. His plan proceeded from the correct premise that to win he must unite the French and American forces and strike at one of the British armies cut off from the other. But the plan had a flaw which might have proved fatal had the Americans seriously pursued it. Washington's error was to imagine he could launch a successful attack on New York.

However, an unforeseen turn of fortune was to alter the whole design and reorder the future course of the war.

Washington knew that Clinton's force was larger than any he and Rochambeau together could muster. He knew, too, the strength of Manhattan's fortifications. But he imagined that he had no alternative. To get at Cornwallis's smaller army called for a long overland march skirting Clinton's stronghold — a march in which the French and Americans would be cut off from their bases and would run the risk of an assault by both British armies.

New York, despite the risks, seemed therefore the necessary goal. Early in July, Washington and Rochambeau joined forces at White Plains and prepared to attack.

Now was chance's first intervention. The advance American detachments sent forward to land secretly upon the island ran into British foraging parties and withdrew. Offered the opportunity for reconsideration by these accidental encounters, the allied generals took more sober stock of their position and reluctantly determined to avoid an engagement that would certainly have proved disastrous.

Their thoughts turned again to Virginia. Perhaps a feint at Yorktown would induce Clinton to reinforce Cornwallis, thus weakening the New York garrison. But the hazards of the move gave them pause.

Long before, Washington had understood that a powerful fleet would give the army mobility. In January, he had sent to Versailles a desperate plea for ships. He had not dared hope that his request would be granted, and since an exchange of letters took five months, he could not afford to wait for a reply. He had been moderately cheered in the late spring by the news that a first-class French fleet under the Comte de Grasse was in the West Indies. But its further moves had then been uncertain.

Early in August, as Washington and Rochambeau lingered indecisively in the vicinity of New York, the long-awaited word came from De Grasse. The French fleet, almost thirty vessels with 3000 additional troops, would sail in the middle of the month for the Chesapeake, prepared to assist in an assault upon Yorktown. The news dispelled every trace of irresolution and brought with it a refreshing certainty of what had to be done. Delighted and relieved, Washington prepared to act.

The pieces of the plan now fell into place. The march to Virginia became feasible when it was clear that supplies could move by sea. A tiny garrison would remain at West Point, while every available man was committed to the gamble of a single decisive campaign. Washington and Rochambeau would steal swiftly across New Jersey and eastern Pennsylvania, while a small fleet under Admiral Barras brought their artillery down from Newport. In September they would all rendezvous with De Grasse in the Chesapeake.

The movement by land was quick and secret, undiscovered by Clinton while he could still intervene. Yet ultimately the fate of the expedition depended upon command of the sea. For a brief interval, but long enough, the French controlled the ocean.

Fortune that spring and summer had mocked Admiral Rodney, the British naval commander in the Atlantic. All year, he had engaged the French in a campaign of "strenuous futility"; indecisive petty fights had sapped his energy. A moody, solitary man, disappointed by his failures, his health had broken down. He had been warned that De Grasse was moving northward, but was reluctant to face the bitter weather of the North Atlantic as autumn advanced. Early in August, as the critical moment of the war approached, Rodney determined to return to England with a part of his fleet for a rest. In any naval battle that was to come, the British would therefore be outnumbered by the larger French force. The balance of power at sea had shifted against them.

They would not intercept the French fleet before it reached the shelter of the Chesapeake or had the opportunity to disembark the troops and equipment for Rochambeau's army. A warning of the danger from De Grasse had indeed been dispatched to Admiral Graves in New York; but the vessel that carried it was lost and never reached port. Not until September 1 did the English ships set sail.

By then De Grasse was safely lodged within the Capes of the Chesapeake ready to greet Graves at his arrival four days later. In the battle that followed, misfortune maintained its attachment to the British. Out-manned and outgunned, surprised that the French were already in occupation, Graves let slip an opportunity to attack before the enemy had formed a line of battle. Thereafter he was doomed to failure. In addition, his signaling system went wrong, or was misunderstood by his subordinates, which only added a comic sting to the defeat.

For the time being, the French were masters of the Bay. Within a week Barras's ships from Newport entered with their precious cargo of artillery, and the armies of Washington and Rochambeau were ferried safely and swiftly from Baltimore and Annapolis to the James near Williamsburg. As September drew to a close, the combined forces were establishing a siege of Yorktown.

Within the beleaguered town, Cornwallis knew soon enough what had happened. A bend in the river cut Yorktown off from a view of the Bay. Yet even from a distance, the naval battle off the Chesapeake must have held Cornwallis's attention. The news of the French victory made grimly clear his own desperate situation. Just over forty at the time, Cornwallis was only at the beginning of a career that would one day earn him distinction in India and Ireland. He had come to America at the very start of the war and had served creditably in the southern theater. Largely through the fault of others, he was about to be responsible for the most decisive defeat in British history.

In the first week of October, the siege settled down to its traditional routine. The French engineers busied themselves mounting the heavy guns, planning trenches, and preparing the apparatus of assault. Occasional sorties and little charges enlivened the long periods of digging and waiting. But mostly it seemed the test would be one of the patience of the attackers against the persistence of the besieged.

Cornwallis was unwilling to surrender. He knew the formidable odds against him and advised Clinton not to attempt to send reinforcements. But there was still a glimmer of hope. Suppose he could break through the trap and escape? Yorktown was surrounded on three sides by the superior forces of the French and Americans. The fourth side was the south bank of the York River.

Cornwallis determined to flee across the river. While the besiegers were still occupied with their digging, he would take his men across in small boats, and then, without baggage or supplies, by forced marches, flee speedily northward to join Clinton. Enough of his army would remain intact to carry on the war.

Late in the night of October 16, the movement began. At midnight, a substantial detachment was across. Then, without warning, a furious storm swept across the river. The boats already over could not come back. Others were carried by the current down the river. For want of a few more hours of calm, of a few more boats, the last hope of escape was gone.

On October 17, Cornwallis offered to surrender.

Surrender at Yorktown removed from the war a substantial portion of the total British armed strength. It also freed a large part of the continent south of New York. Most important, it altered unexpectedly the diplomatic balance upon which Vergennes had counted. Even if the formula proposed by the mediators in the spring were adhered to, it would now have a different meaning. The Americans held far more territory in October than they had six months earlier. However, Yorktown had a wider significance: it was responsible for a shift in control of British politics and, indirectly, gave an entirely new turn to the negotiations then proceeding at Paris.

Yorktown did not make George III any friendlier to the Americans. Bitterly, he insisted he would not recognize the independence of the colonies, and threatened abdication as the preferable alternative. His rage, while genuine enough, now concealed the shift to a new policy.

Although this monarch never was known for the display of tact or common sense, he did have a nose for the realities of a situation. Often enough his choleric outbursts were devices to conceal the embarrassment of an unwelcome accommodation. After Yorktown, there was no alternative to independence; and George III quickly knew it. The news discredited the Tories and the king's friends in power. In the extremity,

George summoned back into office the ministers most friendly to the American cause. Rockingham, who had once earlier repealed the Stamp Act, Shelburne, and Fox were thereafter to make British policy.

The new English ministers had no desire to justify the errors of the past. They preferred to restore friendly relations with the rebellious colonies, not only because they sympathized with the cause, but also to emphasize the shortcomings of earlier Tory policy. Even independence was not too high a price for American friendship, particularly since it would be Lord North, the prime minister responsible for the Revolution, who paid the price.

As the implications of Yorktown sank in through the early months of 1782, the British ministers realized peace was imperative. They held 30,000 troops in North America, consuming enormous quantities of supplies. To maintain and reinforce them would be ruinously expensive. There was no assurance that a new campaign would be any more successful than the old. Most critical, every passing day of war confirmed American dependence upon France. Delay might create for England's traditional enemy a firm friend in the New World.

In March, 1782, therefore, a long series of negotiations looking toward the peace ponderously got under way. The final treaty was not signed for another year. But the essential elements quickly became apparent.

Franklin and Adams were joined in Paris that spring

by a third negotiator, John Jay, come up from Spain where he had fruitlessly been representing the United States. Jay was the youngest of the diplomats, rather vain and self-assured, and very conscious of his gentlemanly upbringing. The unlovely Spanish court in Madrid had left him with a permanent distaste for European statesmanship; and even more than Adams, he was dubious as to Vergennes's intentions.

Jay now uneasily reconsidered the instructions drawn up by the Congress four months before Yorktown. Those instructions reflected a situation that had ceased to exist. The envoys were directed to follow the French minister in all matters; had they literally done as they had been told, they could not long have put off acquiescence in Vergennes's original terms. Yet Jay knew that they could do better and, by dealing with the British, outwit Vergennes. Old family ties and his interests as a spokesman for the New York merchants drew him also to the idea of an Anglo-American accommodation.

There was already a great coming and going of secret agents between London and Paris. Franklin had been dealing with Richard Oswald, an unofficial representative of the English. But in accordance with the rules of the game and with the terms of the French treaty, the Americans had kept Vergennes informed. Jay now found a pretext for cutting short these conversations, and sent to London a secret emissary of his own. The word carried to the new English ministers was that the Americans would consider the framing of a separate preliminary treaty, without the French, and that "it was the obvious interest of Britain immediately to cut the cords which tied us to France."

In November, 1782, the English and Americans agreed upon the terms of settlement that were later written into the treaty of peace. By those terms Franklin, Jay, and Adams secured far more than the most sanguine of them could have dared expect a year earlier. Independence was recognized. The new nation's boundaries reached west to the Mississippi, and the English agreed to evacuate the ports and posts they still held. The Yankees also retained the fishing privileges in British waters they had once held as British subjects. And the United States was not bound to the necessity of compensating the Tories for their confiscated property.

It was no easy matter to break the news of this agreement to the French. When the word came to him, Vergennes took it in silence. For two weeks, he considered the matter, while the American envoys anxiously awaited an indication of his attitude. No doubt Vergennes was offended at having been outmaneuvered; but he was not one to let false pride lead him into headstrong action. His great concern was still to make the best of the unexpected turn in the game.

His reply when it finally came, then, was hardly the bitter protest that might be expected. Reading the moderate note, Franklin knew that the French could be conciliated. In a communication which was a model of tact, the aging Philadelphian admitted that the Americans had perhaps been lacking in *bienséance*, but insisted it was not through want of regard for French interests. The British, he wrote Vergennes, "flatter themselves they have already divided us"; and that warning, he knew, would be enough to remind the king's minister it was necessary to accept the logic of the situation created at Yorktown. On this basis the peace was made.

The other powers fared less well as the remaining issues of the war were settled. France got nothing for all its efforts; Spain received the Floridas in return for the surrender of its hopes for Gibraltar; to the Netherlands were restored some colonies earlier taken from them; and Britain was confirmed in the possession of Canada. But the Americans emerged from the treaty negotiations with the lion's share of the spoils. Although the United States was the weakest of the powers involved, its untrained diplomats had outplayed the professional statesmen of Europe.

More than skill had been responsible. The American envoys had succeeded because they had exploited the situation Yorktown presented. Taking advantage of the British eagerness for peace and Vergennes's anxiety to end the war, they had played one off against the other, and emerged with a highly advantageous settlement. Yet they left England and France eagerly vying for American friendship.

The turning point at Yorktown was the product of the unexpected wanderings of British foragers along the Jersey shore, of the accidental loss of the frigate sent to alert Graves to the presence of the French fleet, of the luck that permitted two separate armies and two separate fleets to converge at the right moment on Yorktown, of the storm that held Cornwallis in the beleaguered town. All these chance events had conspired to make the decisive victory that set to nought Vergennes's most canny plans. As a result, the nation that came into being in 1783 was not the narrow coastal state the Frenchman had envisaged. It had earned a princely territorial settlement within which it could grow in power in the decades of expansion that lay ahead.

CHAPTER TWO

The Louisiana Purchase

AMERICANS faced west in the year 1800. A driving energy had spilled them across the Alleghenies and they now edged over the open plains toward the western extremities of the country. The Mississippi set a limit to the explored territory. Beyond the Mississippi was undisturbed space. In the vast interior of the continent cities would arise, a bountiful soil would yield crops of unparalleled magnitude, and stores of mineral wealth would ultimately come to light. As yet, however, the most fertile imagination could not conceive the future of these immense spaces. Louisiana from the great river to the unknown mountains remained empty. Only the occasional bands of roving Indians disturbed its primeval calm.

Perhaps it was the destiny of this land to be American — to await the conglomerate hosts from New England and the South and from all the ends of Europe who were to make its potentialities real. But without the avarice of a woman, the miscalculations of an emperor, and a trick of the climate, Louisiana might long have remained foreign soil, an imposing barrier in the way of any future thrust to the Pacific.

As the eighteenth century drew to a close, Louisiana was Spanish. It had been handed over to Spain by the French during the French and Indian War as part of the price of alliance. In Madrid little value was put on the new province, except as a kind of buffer state covering the approaches to the northern border of Mexico. Only the city of New Orleans was considered of any importance at all. Here as elsewhere, the Spanish Bourbons were no longer prepared to recognize opportunity in the New World. An inexorable paralysis had settled upon the court, and its lack of ability would shortly lose it the whole of its American empire.

The royal family was foredoomed to futility and knew it. From a description of a royal hunt by the English ambassador, sent back to London, emerges a fleeting insight into the blankness of the Bourbon lives. Before a large crowd, the king, surrounded by his household, stood for hours at the railed enclosures and stolidly pumped bullets into the herd of two thousand deer as the chasseurs drove them in. A little later the pleasures of the chase were further simplified when six fieldpieces, fired at the royal command, relieved the king of the necessity for holding his gun.

In the family portraits, though nowhere else, the monarch, Charles IV, stood in the foreground. He was in his forties when he came to the throne, and the best years of his manhood had been wasted. Neither the regalia of his office nor the elaborate uniforms he occasionally affected could give dignity to his irresolute stance, his paunchy figure, and the sagging muscles of his face.

Charles lived in a constant state of indecision. Conscious of his heritage, he was wrapped up in a ceremonial veneration of the past. The corridors of his mind, like the corridors of his palaces, were packed with the gloomy mementos of a once glorious history. Lost in the dim past, he was disposed to overlook the present.

Yet Charles had strange flashes of awareness of the events that had been shaking Europe for a decade. He respected the achievements of the French Revolution and had unbounded admiration for the young Napoleon, who was now moving to the head of the French state. Charles in fact was torn by conflicting reveries. One minute he dreamed of emulating his ancestors; the next, of putting himself at the head of the new popular forces of revolution. Vacillating between the two courses, he almost never acted of his own accord, but allowed himself to be pushed about as the pawn of others.

He was certainly not the husband for Maria Louisa, his queen. His weak will could hardly curb a woman of violent passions. In this relationship, too, resignation and indecision were his predominant characteristics.

With Maria Louisa herself it was altogether another matter. Born a Bourbon, she had been married to her cousin at the age of fourteen. Essentially of a willful, sensuous nature, she had grasped avidly at pleasure and power. The man in her husband had never satisfied her; although she used fits of jealous temper to keep him under her thumb, she had left herself free to move through a succession of lovers in the court. In Goya's famous portrait of her, she stares out at us, bold and unashamed. There is a coquetry in the glimpse of her tiny shoes, and the jeweled arm that holds a fan is strong and vigorous. Yet the flouncy, low-bosomed gown does not conceal the middle-aged shapelessness of her figure. And her mouth is firmly shut. For by this time Maria Louisa has lost all her teeth; and although the artificial set made for her sparkles with jewels, she prefers to see herself portrayed in the full flush of unblemished youth.

In any earlier era, rigid rules of etiquette and religious sanctions would have set restraints upon the emotions of such a woman. But the revolutionary disturbances in ideas as well as politics had overthrown the world of stable patterns of behavior. Without the guidance of external rules, Maria Louisa became a creature of capricious self-indulgence, prepared for her own gratification to betray both Charles as wife and Spain as queen.

Louisiana was nothing to her; a corner in Italy was more precious than the whole of America. At the moment, her main concern was to find an Italian throne for her brother, the Duke of Parma. Ever since the

French had become the masters of northern Italy she had plotted an accommodation with them that would fulfill her desires. And there were few considerations Maria Louisa allowed to stand in the way of gratification of her desires.

In the entourage of the court she found an ally physically and temperamentally more her type than the indecisive Charles. In the shadows behind both monarchs moved the indistinct figure of Manuel de Godoy. Here indeed was an example of the deterioration in Spanish statesmanship. Godoy had come to Madrid a round-faced boy of seventeen, to serve in the royal Garde de Corps. He had attracted the queen's fancy and, though many years her junior, had become her lover. His devotion was amply rewarded. In 1792, at the age of twenty-five, he became his sovereign's chief minister.

An unprincipled adventurer, Godoy treated men and states as pieces on a chessboard with which he played for his own advantage and for the sake of the game itself. Shrewd enough to know the weakness of his own side, Godoy had correctly assessed the insecurity of the Spanish state as well as the faults of his king and the vanity of his queen. As he made his moves, he kept in mind the positions on the board, but also the possibility that at some point in the game he might prefer to sell out.

What was Louisiana to those who guided the destiny

of the Spanish state? A useless expanse of unknown wilderness, costly to administer and populated only by fifty thousand rude and resentful colonists. In Madrid the territory seemed serviceable only in so far as it might be traded off for some more valuable possession.

By contrast, in the French scheme of things Louisiana had again and again reflected the gleam of imperial dreams. The Mississippi region had been the stake of a great colonial contest that the French Bourbons had bitterly fought and lost. For a century their intrepid soldiers and priests had struggled against desperate odds to link the St. Lawrence, the Great Lakes, and the Mississippi in a vast French dominion reaching from Quebec to New Orleans. The most extravagant hopes had been attached to this truly majestic conception: that the English colonies might be confined to their narrow, precarious coastline; that a thriving French population might grow in Louisiana; and that valuable stores of furs and other raw materials might flow back to enrich the mother country.

Military failures had knocked apart the whole brilliant design. In the successive wars against England, the maritime provinces had been lost, then Canada and the Lakes, and finally Louisiana itself.

Now the French Bourbons were gone, but the old dreams had not disappeared. The revolutionary Directory that had assumed power in 1795 was aggressive and dynamic, determined — out of self-interest and zeal — to expand the power of France. And the English remained foes of the French at every point at which their interests collided. Once again, as the century drew to a close, Louisiana became a factor in the strategic pattern of Anglo-French conflict.

In the war which began in 1793, the French had hoped for American assistance and had been disappointed. The struggling young republic was apparently not ready to sacrifice its own interests out of gratitude for French aid in the War of Independence. On the contrary, it was establishing ever closer ties with England. Jay's treaty of 1795 between the United States and Great Britain revealed the extent to which America had shifted from a French toward an English orientation. Two years later, Yankees and Frenchmen were engaged in undeclared war at sea.

The threat of an Anglo-American alliance, or even of a *rapprochement*, frightened the Directory. Should those two powers draw together, France would confront an unbeatable combination of naval strength. If the Americans could not be won over to an alliance, they must at least be prevented from joining forces with the British.

None knew this better than the new French minister of foreign affairs, Charles Maurice de Talleyrand, who had just returned to France to take up that post after thirty months of exile in the United States. Two careers were already behind him. The younger son of a noble family, he had hobbled through life as a cripple. While he was still a youth, his parents, despairing of a more active future for him, had thrust him into the Church. As Bishop of Autun he had seemed destined to live out his days in the charge of a provincial see, occupying himself with its petty administrative business and enjoying its moderate serenity.

The Revolution had been the opportunity his fierce ambition craved. Flouting convention and disregarding his own clerical position, he had plunged into the violent struggle for political place that followed the collapse of the old regime. But the man was wary; the guillotine piled up too much evidence of the consequences of failure. And although Talleyrand showed a striking ability to recognize the winning side, he had reckoned it healthier to leave the country in 1792.

Before too long, however, he was back, prepared to take a hand in the diplomatic game. Like Godoy, he was not apt to allow conceptions of morality or reasons of state to complicate the rules for him. But unlike Godoy, he played the pieces of a great power. If he had also the finesse and suavity of an experienced player, these characteristics by no means concealed the iron determination with which he made his moves.

Talleyrand had become convinced that the interests of France, and his own, were antithetical to those of the United States. His own stay in the New World had persuaded him that American democracy was a danger to the society of the Old World, and that the manners and customs of the American people would inevitably make them allies of the English. American friendship, he concluded, was of little value, and the expansive tendencies of the Yankees threatened France. The best defense under such circumstances was attack. Possession of Louisiana would give France a base from which to hold the presumptuous Americans in check.

Shortly after the conclusion of Jay's treaty, therefore, the French began to plan the reacquisition of Louisiana. In principle, the Spaniards were quick to consent; by 1796 the draft of a secret treaty was ready. As to the details, however, Godoy and the queen would still have something to say.

Few diplomatic negotiations in the eighteenth century were, after all, concluded as easily as that. Even though both sides agreed as to ends, there was ample opportunity for haggling over the proper terms of payment. In the maneuvering that followed, Talleyrand had the advantage of superior forces. Godoy, on the other hand, could take refuge only in the evasiveness at which he was a master. The bargaining proceeded at a snail's pace throughout the next four years. The French, preoccupied elsewhere, found the Spanish tactics annoying, yet not enough so for an open break; and Godoy, urged on by the queen, continued to hold out for the highest price for Louisiana. The key to these intricate moves was the *pourboire* for Maria Louisa's needy brother, the Duke of Parma.

Of these negotiations the Americans were aware. For them, however, Louisiana was more than a mere pawn on the diplomatic chessboard. The pioneers had come over the mountains, following the river valleys which were their lines of advance to the West. The cleared-out farmlands and the towns along the way were the evidences of their steady progress. But they depended on communication with the outside world for disposal of their raw materials and for the import of those goods that lifted their lives above savagery.

The river system was the vital artery of interior trade for the United States. The mountains cut off all easterly traffic in heavy commodities. Down the Ohio drifted the flatboats and rafts, laden with provisions that were the products of the year's labor of many families. Many a farm lad, perched wide-eyed on the barrels of pork, watched the stream's twisting course, saw it merge with the Mississippi, and found himself, weeks later, entranced by the sight of New Orleans across the marshes.

This was the great metropolis of the West. It held the Americans' imagination because of the fascination of its Creole culture, because of its exotic flavor, and because of the crucial part it played in their economy. For here western produce was unloaded and trans-ferred to the vessels that would carry it over the world. Upon the free flow of goods through this entrepôt hung the welfare of every farm in the West.

New Orleans had always been foreign territory for Americans. But since it guarded the gateway to the Mississippi, the United States had long struggled to

secure trade through the city against arbitrary interruption. In 1795, as the result of an arduous mission
to Madrid, Thomas Pinckney had broken through the
procrastination of the Spanish court and had negotiated a moderately favorable commercial treaty. The
pact recognized the right of Americans freely to navi-
gate the Mississippi, and extended to them the privilege of depositing their goods in New Orleans for
transshipment. These concessions, anxiously anticipated and highly valued in the new Republic, thereafter were fixed points of American diplomacy to be
defended at almost any cost.

As the American envoys in Paris and Madrid got
wind of the dealings that might restore Louisiana to
France, they recognized the threat to the position in
New Orleans that American merchants had laboriously
won. France could resist pressure from the United
States as Spain had not; and the Directory, already hostile, might be tempted to strike at America by choking
off the Mississippi trade. If the cession could not be
avoided, it was of the utmost importance to secure
some advance recognition from the French of the
special American interests in Louisiana.

This atmosphere of relative stalemate persisted
throughout the closing years of the eighteenth century.
In Madrid, in Paris, in Washington, the diplomats continued to compose their crafty notes. Godoy, the
Queen of Spain, Talleyrand, and the succession of

American envoys sent to Paris, weighed their calculating words as if these alone would be decisive. Only along the frontier of Louisiana was there movement, as impatient men sifted in along the border whether the Spaniards wished it or not.

The apparent calm was shattered by the initiative of the most decisive actor in the drama. As the new century began, Louisiana acquired a place in the calculations of Napoleon, the First Consul of France.

Imperial visions had always dazzled the Corsican. As he pondered in retrospect the way he had already come in a decade, his mind leaped ahead in eager expectation to what might be in store for him. The Revolution had made everything possible. It had turned a "corporal" into the ruler of France. It might yet do more.

One dazzling military success after another inflated his dreams, which became increasingly spectacular, and his steadily growing power fixed the image of empire in his ambitious mind.

At first, the empire of his imagination had been situated in the exotic East. Napoleon saw himself as the liberator and master of the fabled Orient, successor to Alexander the Great and the Caesars. But the failure of his Egyptian expedition and the likelihood of conflict with England in that area changed the direction of his thoughts. Now his visions focused upon an American setting. Josephine, herself a Creole, may have fired his imagination with her descriptions of the lush islands set in the azure seas of the Caribbean. Or, it may be, he suddenly realized that the New World might offer more scope for his rising star than the Old. In any case, Napoleon set about building an American empire for France.

Napoleon's vision of a New France differed significantly from that of the Bourbons. It was not to the frozen St. Lawrence or to the remote forests of Canada that Napoleon's mind turned, but to the tropical islands of the West Indies. Santo Domingo was already in his hands. Guadeloupe and Martinique had once been French and could be made so again. And as Spain's hold on her Caribbean possessions weakened, other prizes would readily drop into the grasp of the strongest power on the spot.

In the past, the weakness of these islands had lain in their lack of a continental base. Rich in sugar, they were nevertheless compelled to depend for food and supplies on trade; and their remoteness from France rendered them vulnerable to naval attack. But suppose they were to be supplied with such a base! All the problems of the past would vanish!

It was in this form that Louisiana acquired a place in Napoleon's dreams. His New France would extend its sheltering arms round the whole Gulf of Mexico and the Caribbean, taking in not only the islands but also Louisiana and the Floridas. Resting on a fulcrum at New Orleans, the two great areas of the empire could balance one another. The West Indian islands could produce the tropical staples precious in the markets of Europe. At the same time, a thriving French population in Louisiana could afford the islands military protection and also produce the grains and foodstuffs to feed them. Strong ties of commerce would hold the whole empire together and would attach it economically as well as militarily to France. This creation would be a counterweight to the perennial threat of superior British sea power.

Napoleon proceeded vigorously to make this imaginary empire a reality. The first step was to regain Louisiana.

Napoleon viewed the leisurely diplomatic negotiations in Madrid with impatience. The prospect that Godoy and the queen might continue to draw upon a seemingly endless series of pretexts for delay was intolerable. At Napoleon's insistence, the Spaniards at last agreed to cede Louisiana to the French in the Treaty of San Ildefonso in 1800. This stage of imperial aggrandizement was now complete.

The Americans were immediately affected. The prospect that the territory would shortly fall under Napoleon's control lent urgency to the efforts of the Americans to secure the right of deposit for their goods at New Orleans. A special mission with that objective was now entrusted to Robert R. Livingston of New York sent as minister to France.

Livingston was an excellent choice. He came from a distinguished family and had ably served the state and nation in several capacities. As a member of the Continental Congress, he had organized its department of foreign affairs. Although his name had not been attached to any of the spectacular negotiations of the past, he had had considerable diplomatic experience. More than that, he was animated both by a strong sense of his country's interests and by a feeling for the proprieties. He was attracted to the best in French culture and was as likely as any American to know his way about Paris.

Since his retirement from politics he had been living at Clermont, his estate on the Hudson, where he led the life of a country gentleman, patron of the arts and of agriculture. Without political ambition, he nevertheless understood the importance of the task now assigned him. He assumed the mission as a duty, knowing that its fulfillment would call for his most earnest efforts.

Livingston sailed with instructions either to prevent the retrocession of Louisiana to France, or, failing that, to attempt to purchase New Orleans and West Florida. He had not the least prospect of success. On arriving in Paris, he soon found that his every approach to the foreign ministry seemed doomed to futility. Talleyrand scarcely bothered to be courteous, for there was no likelihood that Napoleon would give up the least part of his holdings in the Caribbean.

Indeed, the First Consul's determination to establish his American empire was stronger than ever. The peace that was made with England in 1801 restored to France the West Indian islands which the British had previously captured. At the same time, an imposing expedition of twenty thousand men under General Leclerc was dispatched to restore order in Santo Domingo, where the violent Negro uprising under Toussaint L'Ouverture had by now run its course. By a combined display of force and cajolery the French were finally able to reach an understanding with the leaders of the Blacks. There remained only the matter of taking actual possession of Louisiana, of establishing a government there, and of making the territory permanently French. To this task, too, Napoleon energetically devoted himself.

In the summer of 1802, Napoleon prepared a great expedition to cross the Atlantic and to plant the French flag in New Orleans. In Holland, on the River Scheldt, a sizable armada of ships, thousands of soldiers, and vast stores of equipment were gathered under General Victor. In all, some 2 million francs were expended in the effort.

The expedition readied itself during the summer at the little Dutch town of Helvoet Sluys. But the occasions for delay seemed almost endless. Materials were difficult to come by and were assembled slowly. Then, it seemed, no definite sailing date could be set, because the Spanish court continued its intolerable evasive tactics and had not yet actually issued the order to cede the territory to the French. Godoy and Maria Louisa apparently had not yet come to the end of their efforts to extort the maximum price in the bargain. Not until the middle of October, 1802, fully two years after the treaty had been signed, were the minister and the queen compelled to yield. At that point, General Victor's expedition was instructed to prepare to depart.

Godoy's evasive tactics had proved costly for the French. The months spent in waiting for action from Madrid had seen the summer and fall go by. Now the northern winter was beginning to close in. General Victor hastened his final preparations. One morning, as he was almost in readiness, he woke to find an advancing edge of frost moving across the harbor of Helvoet Sluys. Before he could act, the whole expedition was icebound.

The Dutch winter and the ice lasted through January and February, while Victor's men consumed the supplies that should have carried them to Louisiana. Sitting idly in their quarters, the French commanders still planned the occupation and the government of the new territory; and when spring released the harbor from the grip of ice, the fleet once more prepared to set sail.

A violent storm occasioned a new delay of two weeks. But at last, in April, the troops were embarked. The pilots boarded the ships and were on the point of taking the fleet through the estuary to the open waters when a halt was called. Word had come that a courier bore dispatches from Paris. General Victor now learned to his amazement that the whole expedition had been recalled. Louisiana had been sold to the Americans. The delay had altered the plans of his government.

In Paris, the months had gone fruitlessly by for Livingston, idle against his will. He made no perceptible progress in his mission. In October, 1802, he had reached an impasse from which there was no apparent exit. Then, too, the whole problem was complicated by an act of deliberate mischief on the part of Godoy — an act directed against Napoleon but one that injured mostly the Americans.

Godoy had come bitterly to resent the pressure put on him by the French; and the queen not too delicately played upon his wounded vanity. Maria Louisa had been granted her Italian lands. But they were not the provinces for which she had hoped. Furthermore, they went not to her brother but to her nephew; nor had they yet actually been handed over. In the whole transaction, Maria Louisa and Godoy felt that Napoleon had been highhanded and arbitrary. Subtly they found an occasion for getting back at the First Consul by embroiling him with the Americans. If France was to have Louisiana, let it be with as many vexing problems as possible. A few days after Spain ordered the cession of Louisiana to the French, the governor at New Orleans, no doubt at Godoy's instigation, withdrew the right of deposit accorded the Americans by Pinckney's treaty.

For the farmers of the West, this was disastrous. Colonial produce could no longer float down the inland waters and be transshipped at New Orleans for export. The gates to the open world had been slammed shut. This was a blow not only at American trade but at America's capacity to expand. Although the privilege was before long restored, the incident revealed dramatically that the Americans were right to fear their dependence upon an alien power at the mouth of the Mississippi. His earlier experiences with Talleyrand gave Livingston little ground for the belief that the French might be more tractable or more considerate of American interests.

Livingston had offered to pay 20 million francs for New Orleans and Florida. As an alternative, he was willing to let New Orleans become a free port. But he was still not hopeful that either proposal would be accepted, although James Monroe was on his way to assist in the negotiations. Yet as the winter passed in casual interchanges with Talleyrand, he found the rebuffs fewer. His suggestions were received with moderate politeness, and somehow conversations drifted to discussions of concrete terms. This was the most encouraging sign the Americans had yet had.

The change in attitude reflected a change in Napoleon's plans. The ice that held his ships in the harbor at Helvoet Sluys altered his view of the whole situation. The winter went by and his American empire was no nearer reality. In January came disastrous news from the West Indies. Yellow fever had stricken General Leclerc's army, swept away a substantial part of his manpower, and left him open to a defeat by the resurgent Negroes. The troops that should by then have been available in Louisiana to reinforce him were still in Holland. To establish the New World colony would now entail higher cost, more imposing difficulties than anyone had imagined a few months back.

Napoleon's finance minister, François Barbé-Marbois, was himself a Creole and knew at first hand the difficulties of establishing control in Santo Domingo. For years he had labored to bring order into the fiscal affairs of the French state, and his calculating mind was distressed by the prospect of new expenditures. Millions of francs would have to be devoted to a new expedition. Was it worth the cost?

It was Napoleon's strength neither to admit defeat nor to be trapped by stubborn adherence to a ruinous course. When confronted by a mistake, he had the consoling capacity to persuade himself that it was something else he had really wanted all along. So now, as the difficulties of establishing an American empire became clear, he concluded that the stakes were too high. His thoughts shifted back to Europe. Why should not his empire be in the Old World rather than the New? Shortly he would become emperor of the French, and already he was thinking of the entire continent as his domain.

Louisiana suddenly became a useless encumbrance. Napoleon might have restored it to the Spaniards. But the actions of the court in Madrid had so antagonized him that any alternative seemed preferable. It was almost certain that his developing European ambitions would embroil him in difficulties with the English. And in the new war which would shortly break forth, there might be some value to American good will. In March, 1803, he determined to hand over the whole of Louisiana to the Americans.

Talleyrand waited until April to act. Then, in the midst of a casual conversation with Livingston, he proposed the sale of the whole territory. It took the startled envoy only a few minutes to leap at the suggestion, once he was sure his ears had not deceived him. Before the month was over, before General Victor could leave Helvoet Sluys, Louisiana was American for some fifteen million dollars.

The vast expanse between the Mississippi and the mountains was thus joined to the young American republic. President Jefferson realized at once the import of the windfall. Certainty as to the necessity of the purchase overcame whatever doubts he may have had as to his constitutional powers to effect it.

Shortly Lewis and Clark and Zebulon Pike would penetrate the unknown spaces of the territory. After them would come the bands of trappers and traders, and at last the numberless legions of husbandmen. Thanks to the ice that had formed across the waters of a remote Dutch harbor, the advancing host of American settlers moving westward towards the Pacific at a turning point in our history now found the way open before them.

CHAPTER THREE

Explosion on the *Princeton*

THE chill of early morning had not yet left the air, when the man-of-war *Princeton* moved down the Potomac on February 28, 1844. She was the pride of the American Navy, a steamer fitted with an Erricsson propeller. Launched scarcely six months earlier, she had already demonstrated her speed by outracing the famous British liner of steam and sail, the *Great Western*. On this day her commander, Captain Stockton, was to make another display of her power.

Aboard were a distinguished group of passengers. President Tyler and his most important military and naval advisers, along with a select group of politicians, had come to observe a trial of the *Princeton's* new gun, the "Peacemaker," an immense twelve-inch piece, fully sixteen feet long, capable of throwing a 225-pound ball. (Why the gun had been named the "Peacemaker" and what irony was concealed in its title would not be clear for many years to come.)

With the President was his Secretary of State. Abel P. Upshur was a Virginian recently elevated to the post; he had a particular interest in the trip, for as the former

Secretary of the Navy he had watched the development of this new piece of ordnance.

The pleasant cruise proceeded some distance below Fort Washington and on the way the *Princeton* fired several bursts to the satisfaction of all. The ladies took a "sumptuous repast" in the captain's cabin, and then it was the turn of the gentlemen at the table. Bottles were passed and a goodly number of toasts were drunk. The President was in genial humor, and noticeably attentive to pretty Julia Gardiner. Thirty years his junior, she was soon to be his bride.

As dusk descended several of the distinguished guests drifted back to the deck, where they stood in little groups, relaxed in easy conversation, watching the shore slip by.

Those who had remained behind in the cabin were suddenly surprised to hear another gun go off; the dull explosion seemed prolonged. There was a moment of silence; then screams could be heard of men in agony and the sound of running feet overhead. The visitors hastened to the deck, where they were alarmed to see the ship's surgeon desperately working over a group of bodies, one of them covered with a flag. The "Peacemaker" had exploded; several bystanders had been killed — and among them was Secretary of State Upshur, who had come up with the Secretary of the Navy to witness one last test of the gun.

Upshur had been well liked; he was capable, a man

of few enemies; and the ship's company were left in horrified silence. With the mourning at the personal loss, there were mingled other more general forebodings. Who would now carry forward the momentous negotiations in which the Secretary of State had been engaged? How would the incident affect the presidential election, less than a year away? How would it influence the delicate balance of power that held the contending sections of the nation together?

Time would confirm the uneasy misgivings of that tragic day. On the distant plains of Texas, on the arid battlefields of Mexico, and in the bloody conflicts of the Civil War, Americans would discover the distant consequences of the failure of the "Peacemaker."

When Upshur had last left his desk, he had been preoccupied with the affairs of Texas. His successor would inherit a sadly tangled web of problems involving American relationships with that young republic.

Citizens of the United States had long viewed the great southwestern province with acquisitive interest. Beyond the farthest limits of their own country, it had lain vast and uninhabited on the road to the fabled wealth of Mexico. Enterprising Yankees had here and there penetrated its desolate reaches in search of commerce and adventure. Remote from the centers of government, with all boundaries and jurisdictions vague and undefined, Texas had for decades been a magnet for all sorts of trading and filibustering expeditions.

Twice in the first twenty years after 1800 Americans had been involved in abortive revolutions along the long, indented coast of the Gulf of Mexico. In 1812 a former Army officer named Augustus Magee, on the lookout for a likely chance, had joined forces with a Mexican exile, Bernardo Gutiérrez. The two had been inspired by the disorders endemic to all Latin America to hope they might carve a principality for themselves out of the collapsing Bourbon empire. They led a small force into Texas, and won some initial victories. Then total defeat by the Spaniards exterminated their invading force and put a disastrous end to their visions of conquest.

While Mexico fought for its own independence, the filibusterers again tried their luck. Out of Mississippi came James Long, leader of a spirited band of frontiersmen determined to make Texas their west, and not above summoning Jean Lafitte, the pirate, to their aid to do so. At Nacogdoches they proclaimed a republic and rode daringly into the interior to make good their pretensions. Long, too, met his defeat and death at the hands of the Mexicans.

Meanwhile the United States had renounced its own vague claims to the territory. That, with the failure of the successive uprisings, seemed to put the whole region safely in the hands of the new Mexican Republic, which had achieved its independence in 1821.

Acceptance of these political conditions did not,

however, hold back the American settlers. Sharp-eyed men, toughened by the wilderness, self-reliant through experience, and accustomed to making their interests one with their rights, were turning the possibilities of acquisition over in their minds. They believed that Texas was theirs, for the bidding.

One of these was Moses Austin. A Yankee trader from Connecticut, he had come south to Richmond after the Revolution; but the little town did not offer him the opportunity he sought. The West, unrevealed and unexploited, seemed full of promise, the more attractive to Austin as his disappointments made him dissatisfied with his petty trader's life. In the 1790's he was off to Missouri, which was then still Spanish, and there, for nearly two decades, he drifted in and out of one unsuccessful enterprise after another. Well, by then his time was running out. He still thought himself young, and unobtrusively subtracted six years from his age. He never lost his formality on the frontier; decent broadcloth and white shirt testified to his Yankee antecedents. Yet there were signs of worry in his deepset eyes beneath the high brow. As his sixtieth birthday drew near, his heart sank with the realization that he might after all wind up a failure. Only in the empty spaces of the farther West, in Texas, was there one more chance of a happy ending to a long career of aimless striving. His determination fastened on that hope.

In 1820, he hastened to Bexar (San Antonio), carry-

ing a grandiose scheme for a colony on which he promised to plant three hundred families. Perhaps the inten-
sity of his longing lent conviction to his plea; or his
plan was in accord with the ambitions of the local
officials, among whom he found an old friend. In any
case, Austin carried back to Missouri with him the
promise of the cherished land grant. He died almost
at once on his return, worn out by his efforts. But the
prize, long elusive, was his.

The burden of carrying forward the project fell to
his son, Stephen F. Austin. The young man was cut
from an altogether different cloth. Born in Virginia,
Stephen Austin had been brought up in the rough-and-
tumble of Southern frontier life. He had followed his
father's wanderings to the Southwest, and was no
stranger to the plains. He was not a handsome man,
but his high forehead and deep eyes gave him
an air of earnestness and integrity. Everywhere, his
patience and tact and a kind of relaxed ability to get
on with any man stood him in good stead. He was only
twenty-seven when Moses died, but he had already
been active in territorial politics, and had served a
term as circuit judge in Arkansas.

In 1821 Stephen Austin fitted out and himself led
to the banks of the Brazos a company who became the
first permanent settlers in Texas from the United States.
What was more, with infinite tolerance for the pro-
crastinating inclinations of Mexican officials, he secured
confirmation of the grants in return for the agreement

to people them. He thus opened the way to further concessions to still other Americans.

In the next few years a little enclave of *norteamericanos* established itself in the province. In the region between the Sabine and the Nueces Rivers, the government of Mexico handed over to the newcomers a succession of grants, each as much as eleven square leagues in size. The *empresarios* who took possession agreed to establish one hundred families on the land; and, although they were far from meeting this obligation, a stream of settlers moved into the area. By 1830 Texas could boast of a total population of perhaps 20,000, almost all migrants from the United States.

From the start there was trouble. The rude, self-confident frontiersmen clashed all too often with officials accustomed to the more leisurely ways of an easier society. Control of the state of Coahuila-Texas was in the hands of officials appointed from Mexico City. But the Americans had their own organ of local government in the *ayuntamiento*. The newcomers were not accustomed to give much regard to the punctilios of law, and consequently ran frequently afoul of the elaborate Mexican codes. The *empresarios* were bound by obligations to the government of Mexico, but the farmers they induced to migrate had no such responsibilities. Some of the settlers, coming out of the South, had brought Negro slaves with them, hoping to establish cotton culture on the fertile soil. Others aspired to import slaves and to create a plantation system. True, a

Mexican law of 1824 forbade the importation of slaves; but the rising demand offered a convincing reason for forgetting a law that no one enforced.

Nor were the *empresarios* and the other settlers more likely to heed the letter of Mexican law with regard to religion. They were Protestants, but by their coming had tacitly agreed to take on the established religion of the country. Yet none of them took the obligation seriously.

On these and other scores there were clashes now and then between the new settlers and the government, the bitterness of which was tempered for the time being only by the fact that the center of authority was remote; the federal government was itself insecure and unwilling to bring issues to a head.

Nevertheless, the crisis was not long postponed. In 1826 a hot-headed *empresario,* Haden Edwards, rose in rebellion and proclaimed the Fredonian Republic. Edwards was not one of Austin's followers. A firebrand, he was not a man to command the confidence of his fellows; he failed to gain support, and, yielding to a repressive expedition from Mexico City, fled to Louisiana.

The uprising, vain though it was, frightened the Mexican administration. The specter of Yankee conquest grew to haunt the timorous rulers of the Republic. The *empresarios* were growing steadily in numbers; and who could tell but that they were plotting with the government of the United States to secure the transfer of the province? Confirmation of these fears could indeed be found in events across the border. A newspaper campaign by expansionists in the United States openly announced the necessity for acquiring Texas; and President Jackson in 1829 actually explored the possibility of purchasing the province.

Gloomily surveying the prospect, from on the spot, was an emissary from Mexico City, General Manuel de Mier y Teran, Commandant General of the Eastern Provinces of Mexico and responsible for the defense of Texas. Mier y Teran, now middle-aged, was a man of scientific interests who had been drawn into the Mexican revolution by patriotic fervor. He was determined to maintain the integrity of his country. Given to spells of melancholia that would one day drive him to suicide, he could not understand the raw frontier society that surrounded him. This courtly man, who loved order and decent regard for form, looked somberly upon the strange mixture of people pouring across the border. He resented the lack of respect for government and the violation of law that he found everywhere, and he was impatient with religious laxity.

Above all, he feared "the most avid nation in the world" to the north. That power, he warned, had already "by silent means," and without "armies, battles, or invasions," laid hands on a great part of the continent. It threatened now to encroach upon Mexican soil, and the *empresarios*, who were its vanguard, had to be restrained in the interests of national security.

Upon his recommendation, the Mexican Congress in 1830 forbade further colonization by citizens of the United States. At the same time, it encouraged Mexicans and Europeans to move in and provided for the military defense of the territory.

Smoldering dissatisfaction with this state of affairs finally broke out in a local revolt in Galveston in 1832. A minor skirmish deposed the commander of the garrison but left the immediate region in a state of revolt.

At this point, the cause of Texas became bound up with the career of Antonio López de Santa Anna. Almost forty at the time, Santa Anna had already had a tempestuous career. He had abandoned the business into which his family had put him — he was not destined, he said later, to be a "counter-jumper" — and had taken up the profession of arms. In the struggle for Mexican independence, he had first been a royalist. Then he had turned against his Spanish masters and had risen fast under the new government. Vain, without scruples or sense of humanity, his romantic ambition had no limits. He was able when he wished to be, but he was often incapable of disciplining his abilities. At the time of the Galveston revolt he made a contested election the pretext for mutiny, and he encouraged the Americans around Galveston in their rebellion.

Santa Anna was not a theorist; intensely ambitious, he grasped at whatever chance seemed likely to add to his power. Aspiring to the presidency, he discovered a useful slogan in states' rights. His vague statements about decentralization encouraged the Texans to believe that, under his administration, they could attain some sort of autonomous position within the Mexican Republic.

Santa Anna no sooner gained power — the Mexican Congress recognized him as President in 1833 — than he forgot even the shadowy promises he had earlier made. Instead he introduced a series of repressive measures against the American settlers, more restrictive than those of his predecessors. In 1835 he was responsible for the enactment of a law that centralized the administration of the whole country, and crushed the vestiges of states' rights. The hopes of the Texans for autonomy as a Mexican state died that year.

The self-government denied them under the Mexican Republic they now sought outside it. For several years groups of Texans had been meeting in conventions to petition for redress of their grievances and the reform of their government. Stephen F. Austin and the *empresarios* had exercised a moderating influence in these gatherings. Become conservative as they had become wealthy, they were conscious of their debt to Mexico and anxious for an accommodation that would keep the country intact and yet meet the more pressing demands of the other Americans in Texas.

Santa Anna's repression of federalism was the last straw. A "consultation" or convention had already been scheduled to meet at New Washington on the Brazos in

October, 1835. When it assembled, its members determined to take up arms in resistance. Yet even here
the conservatism of Austin made itself felt. Fearful
lest the convention move "too fast and too far," he
persuaded that body to adopt as its aim the restoration
of constitutional government within the Mexican Republic.

Alas, Santa Anna's callousness put to nought all the
results of Austin's tact. The "consultation" had created
a provisional state government and had adjourned to
meet again in March, 1836. Before that date arrived,
news came of the battle at the Alamo.

In the little mission in San Antonio, 188 Americans
under W. B. Travis had been cooped up by an army
of 5000. The men who stood siege had come a long
way to this little outpost up the river. They had come
in their faith that this West was American, and would
be their home. At whatever cost they were determined
to cling to that faith. And that involved resistance,
without compromise, to any infringement of their
rights as free men. They had no illusions as they issued
a defiant call for help to "all Americans in the world";
above the cathedral they could see the black flag of No
Quarter. But they would not yield, though they knew
they were cut off from every hope of aid.

For a few days they held off the attackers. Then, exhausted, their supplies gone, they still did not surrender. As Santa Anna's army swarmed over the walls
to the sound of the *degüello* (the beheading call), they

fought on in hand-to-hand conflict, and died in silent fury. No quarter was asked or given; three women, two children, and a Negro servant survived.

After the Alamo even Austin recognized that no further connection with Mexico was tolerable; independence for Texas was the only possible course. The provisional government proclaimed itself a sovereign state and prepared to fight to make the proclamation successful.

To proclaim a nation was easy enough; to give it life and vigor to defend itself was another matter. Santa Anna had every intention of snuffing out this uprising. It would take courage, energy, and skill to resist.

Responsibility for guiding the Texans through this crisis fell to an aging comrade-in-arms of Andrew Jackson. Sam Houston had been born in Virginia of the same Scotch-Irish stock as "Old Hickory." He, too, had served in the War of 1812, and like Jackson had moved into Tennessee politics. A striking figure, six feet two in height, Houston had become adept as a stump speaker and had made himself Congressman and Governor. When he married Eliza Allen, a woman of wealth, grace, and social position, he had been well on the way to establishing himself in the new Southern aristocracy.

Then, he had given it all up. He could not accommodate himself to the lady who was his wife. She left him and Houston at once sensed a bitter discontent with everything he had become. By the divorce he

lost his home, his status, and his place in politics. He
turned to the West and sought refuge in the Indian
country, among the nomadic tribesmen of the plains.
In a gesture of rejection he took a new wife from
among the Indians and was himself adopted by the
Cherokees. In the next few years he led a dissolute
life, trading in a small way, carousing with his Tiana,
existing without ambition or purpose.

In 1833 Houston had had some contacts with the
Texans, who had been impressed with his military reputation. Their admiration stirred the embers of his
self-respect, of the desire for fame. When the crisis
deepened, the new republic called upon him to be its
commander-in-chief. Rekindled ambitions finally induced him to heed the summons; and it was he who
led the way to Texan independence.

By the best standards of military science, Houston
was not much of a general. His strategy was simple —
to wait, like the Indians, for the opportunity for am-
bush or surprise and then to strike in one merciless
blow that would avenge the martyrs of the Alamo and
repel the immediate threat to Texas. Something less
than one thousand men had gathered under his stand-
ard, rough and untrained, but imbued with a fierce
desire to destroy the invader. With this army Houston
drew back into the interior, knowing the Mexicans
would not hasten to follow.

President Santa Anna himself was in command of
the federal Mexican troops. Victory at the Alamo com-

ing after earlier, lesser skirmishes had bolstered his
confidence and given him an occasion for celebration.
He had no great respect for the fighting power of the
yanquis; and so the celebration prolonged itself. He
moved in leisurely pursuit, dividing his attentions between a beautiful young mistress he had acquired en
route and desultory plundering of the homes of terror-
ized settlers.

In mid-April, Houston struck without warning.
Forced marches, in little more than two days, brought
his army back the fifty-five miles to New Washington.
There Santa Anna was encamped without a suspicion
that the Texans were anywhere within reach, without
even sentries on guard. A sudden attack threw the
President into a panicky withdrawal that left him the
next afternoon trapped in the swamps of the San Ja-
cinto River. Houston then hit the Mexicans again at
the siesta hour, while Santa Anna was asleep. When
the battle ended, six Texans and more than six-hun-
dred Mexicans were dead, and the President himself
was Houston's prisoner. The independence of Texas
was assured. After a brief captivity, Santa Anna, who
valued his own skin above all, was released on condi-
tion he withdraw Mexican troops from the new republic.

For the United States, Texan independence posed
an embarrassing problem. Jackson had earlier wished
this area to be part of the Union. But he had hesitated,
unwilling to antagonize Mexico and conscious that new

territory might disturb the delicate balance of political power in the United States. He and Van Buren, his successor, thought it wise, for the time being, simply to recognize Texan independence and to proceed slowly to eventual annexation.

Caution became still more necessary in 1840 when the Whig Party came to power. Daniel Webster, who played a leading role in the new administration, had earlier opposed annexation; influential groups in the North feared, with him, that the addition of new Southern states might weaken New England's power in Congress. Moreover, the United States was then negotiating with Great Britain the ticklish disputes over the northern boundaries of Oregon and Maine. Any precipitous step toward annexation might antagonize London.

Britain too had long been interested in the territory. For two decades English statesmen had been encouraging the Latin-American states in their struggle for freedom. In their view, Texas was similarly to be sustained.

Furthermore, Texas, they hoped, might be the field for an interesting experiment. English factories consumed cotton in large and growing quantities. Yet it was galling to be dependent for that staple on the slave-tilled fields of the South. The abolition of slavery in the British West Indies a few years earlier had demonstrated that other tropical crops could be raised with free labor. Might not Texas be the occasion for a similar trial with cotton?

Houston, for one, was not bound by any particular attachment to the United States, and was quite willing to turn to England for support. Although the majority of Texans probably leaned towards the Union, they were not willing to wait indefinitely, anxious, at the door. It was altogether conceivable they might accept as an alternative an understanding by which Great Britain would recognize the Republic, as France already had in 1839. Great Britain might also guarantee the independence of Texas, and, by loan or subsidy, enable it to free its slaves and establish itself on a firm financial basis.

So, at least, ran the fears of President Tyler. Tyler, too, was a Virginian. His long record as a states' rights Democrat had not prevented him from entering into a temporary alliance with the Whigs in the election of 1840. As a candidate for the vice-presidency he had been expected to cut into Democratic votes and to be amply rewarded by the tenure of a dignified but innocuous position. He was then distinctly the silent partner of the "Tippecanoe and Tyler, too" campaign.

The death of President Harrison shortly after the inauguration had altered the situation. Tyler became chief executive, and he unexpectedly displayed both an unwillingness to act the figurehead and the desire to run again in 1844. For three years he played a difficult role battling factions of both parties, antagonizing many members of the Senate and House, and governing by a *de facto* coalition of his own supporters.

As the presidential year, 1844, approached, Tyler attempted to reassess his own position. The Whigs were decisivly alienated. He could aspire to a second term only with Democratic support. But since the party leaders were hostile, he could attract that support only by identifying himself with some popular issue. There, in his mind, lay the significance of Texas. On that question he could draw upon the deep wells of expansionist sentiment throughout the country — enough to carry him once more to the White House. The Webster-Ashburton Treaty had settled the outstanding disputes with Great Britain. Relieved of those burdens, Tyler felt free to pursue the Texan negotiations. He broke with Webster whom he had kept in office to conclude the English negotiations, and appointed the Virginian, Upshur, as Secretary of State in place of the godlike Daniel.

From Tyler's point of view the diplomatic key to the negotiations was the assurance to the Texans that the United States would protect them in the event that Mexico should resume the attack. It was equally important that annexation be consummated without stirring up the slavery controversy. Were the question to become one of slavery against freedom, the two-thirds majority necessary to ratify a treaty in the Senate could not be secured. The occupation, independence, and annexation of Texas, therefore, had to be treated as what it had in fact been, a stage in the process of expansion, unrelated to slavery.

In the desire to put the matter in terms of manifest destiny, Tyler had the cooperation of responsible statesmen of both parties. Clay and Van Buren, the presumptive Whig and Democratic candidates, issued statements — perhaps timed to come out together — that were intended to soothe potential fears. And Upshur, as Secretary of State, was carrying out discreet, secret negotiations to complete the diplomatic arrangements without heated public debate. Had Upshur lived to carry through the plans already formed, Texas might have come into the Union without the blaze of controversy that actually followed its admission.

The explosion aboard the *Princeton* vacated the office of Secretary of State and placed in new hands the conclusion of the dealings with Texas.

In the choice of a successor to Upshur, Tyler confronted a difficult decision. The political crisis and the approaching election narrowly restricted the range of possible candidates. Since Tyler had himself broken with both parties, he could not approach any of the recognized party leaders. Nor were any of them likely to accept office in a dying administration without popular or Congressional support. Only one man equally isolated would throw in his lot with the President. That man was John C. Calhoun.

Calhoun was now approaching the inglorious twilight of his career. At sixty-two, he had lost every important battle and alienated every colleague. As he sat in Washington, cut off from his family, his anxious thoughts would drift back to the wife whom he loved, yet who punished him with frenetic fits of "nerves" for his absorption in a career which she jealously hated. He could not derive much satisfaction from his past accomplishments. The old man, tired, no longer thought in terms of personal advancement. Every position short of the nation's highest office he had already held — in South Carolina, in the Senate, in the cabinet, as well as the vice-presidency. And his ambitions for the presidency he had surrendered. He had no wish to be Tyler's rival, nor any compunctions about accepting office.

Now he looked bitterly at a country he had helped to make but which he no longer recognized. Thirty years earlier, he too had seen the vision of a great nation, free and expansive. In the intervening decades, however, he had made much too many wrong choices. Now it was too late to act; all that remained was apologia.

In the last years of his life, Calhoun devoted his best energies to the justification of his lost causes. His superb brain had twisted its way through many disputes; he could now turn it to support any argument. As his horizons crowded in upon him, Calhoun fixed his attention ever more on the defense of his own State and his own section, knowing in his inner heart they were doomed with all else that he cherished. "The South! The poor South!" he was to murmur as he died. Yet, he was forever wiping away his sense of guilt about his desertion of the national ideals that had so moved him in his young manhood.

Always he came back to slavery. It was that institution that had driven a wedge between the North and South, that had deprived him of the presidency. Slavery had led the South away from the path the North had taken, away from the visions Calhoun once had glimpsed. But this cast-iron man was incapable of admitting error in himself or seeing tragedy in the history of his section. Slavery could not have been wrong, nor the least action taken in its defense! That defiant judgment he would reiterate with every resource of logic his tortuous mind could uncover, even if it meant denial of the terms of progress accepted elsewhere in the Western world. His personal, social, and intellectual commitments by 1844 drove him to an inflexible dogmatism: slavery was necessary, indeed, beneficient, indeed, a good and proper institution in itself; South Carolina had come the right way, while the rest of the world was steeped in error.

For Calhoun, Texas was of transcendent importance. It was the occasion to demonstrate that slavery was not a dying, anachronistic vestige of the past, but rather a living, creative, expansive institution, not doomed to retreat but to spread. It was more than time to shift away from the defensive stand conservative Southern politicians had taken, and to assume the aggressive posture worthy of the civilization the South defended.

Calhoun's first thoughts as Secretary of State were of Texas. The proposed treaty was in good shape, with all the essential points agreed upon in earlier conversations with the Texan commissioner. But before him was a note from Lord Aberdeen, the British Foreign Secretary, commenting on his government's interest in Texas. The document closed with assurances that England had no intention of interfering in American domestic affairs, but added a conventional statement of interest in the extension of freedom throughout the world.

Calhoun deliberately made this statement the occasion for a tart retort to dramatize the issue as he saw it. He went far beyond the immediate necessity of the argument to a general, abstract defense of slavery as a positive good. Widely circulated, his answer brought into the open the controversy that every other American statesman had tried to repress.

The immediate results were confusing. Northerners who might have voted to join Texas to the Union could not now assent to the addition of another slave state; the treaty was defeated in the Senate.

Texas figured prominently in the election of 1844. Tyler was passed over in the choice of candidates. Van Buren, for his antislavery predilections, was rejected by the Democratic party; and Clay, wavering between North and South, could not take a position strong enough to appeal to either section. The victory went to Polk, an expansionist who had made clear his Southern, proslavery sympathies. And the election was no sooner over than annexation was consummated through a joint resolution of Congress that brought Texas in — a slave state.

What followed was almost anticlimactic, as many Americans had foreseen it would be. The Mexicans recognized neither the independence of Texas nor its annexation by the United States. But their stubborn pride was tempered by caution, and they were not likely except through intransigence to resist the course of events.

But by now Texas was no longer the issue. Further west toward the Pacific lay what is now California and New Mexico, and some Americans were already considering the acquisition of all Mexico. That state was not eager for battle. But a feint at the border in 1846 provoked it into fighting; and when the short war reached its foregone conclusion, the United States stretched in an unbroken mass westward across the continent. The expansive forces that had led its people across the Ohio, then beyond the Mississippi into Louisiana, and then onward into Texas, had fulfilled their manifest destiny.

Political debate had veered away from territorial expansion, however. At the turning point in 1844, when the new Secretary of State had taken Upshur's place, the dark problem of slavery inherited from the nation's past had come to absorb all men's attention. Calhoun's intervention had united inextricably the future of slavery and of westward expansion. The efforts of Clay, Van Buren, and Benton to keep the questions apart were decisively frustrated. Thereafter there could be no evading the question. In any further additions of territory, would slavery, as of right, march with the American flag or not?

Many respectable Northerners began to wonder whether there was not after all some point to the inflammatory preachings of the abolitionists. Earlier it had been easy to write off the antislavery agitators as irresponsible fanatics. Moderate men kept clear of their disorderly proceedings, their endless internal dissensions, their unrestrained invective. The question left by the Mexican War, however, called attention to the heated oratory of the reformers' meeting halls. Did not the progression of events from Calhoun's note to Lord Aberdeen to the acquisition of the southwestern territories indeed prove the existence of a slaveholders' conspiracy? The number of committed abolitionists still remained small. But there was a rapid growth in the number of citizens determined that slavery must not be permitted to spread beyond its present borders.

In Pennsylvania young David Wilmot, a Democratic Congressman, pondered the question and decided that there could, in all conscience, be no answer but the negative. When the occasion presented itself in 1848, Wilmot proposed, in a proviso to an appropriations bill, that the new territories acquired from Mexico be forever free and totally closed to slavery. The Compromise of 1850 did not close the debate thus started, nor the Kansas-Nebraska Bill of 1854. Rather it dragged on through the bloody battlefields of Kansas and was protracted in the convention halls in which the Southern states, in 1861, enacted their ordinances of secession. As it developed, the existing political parties collapsed and a tragic cleavage opened between the two sections of the nation.

At long last there would come a spring day in Charleston harbor when the Carolina gentry would come down to watch the guns booming across the bay at the little island over which the Stars and Stripes still waved. The shells that fell around Fort Sumter in 1861 had long before been touched off by the explosion of the "Peacemaker" on the *Princeton*. For it was then that the issue had been drawn, whether the future of the country would be one of growing freedom or spreading slavery.

CHAPTER FOUR

Fourth of July at Gettysburg

ON July 3, 1863, young Henry Adams wrote home from the English capital. He was tired. He wished the letter to be gay, but the words came slowly; a tone of despondency crept into the phrases that described the events of the past few days.

A round of festivities had left him little time for sleep. Each morning he went for a long ride in the park, worked a bit in the afternoon, then stayed out to dinner until late in the evening. On Monday he had attended a dance in the afternoon and a ball that began at 11:30 at night. On Tuesday he had been a guest at the most magnificent ball of the London season.

This was the life of a young English gentleman. As Henry wrote it down, he could well imagine the envy — or contempt — of his brothers and friends on the other side of the ocean.

But there was ever a bitter potion mixed in with the pleasuresome brew of which he drank. For it was not after all to be a gay blade that he had come to Great Britain. His mission was more serious. Sent off to London with his father before secession had led to war, he had not the opportunity to bear arms himself. But fully as earnestly as those who stood in the ranks of the Army of the Potomac, he was fighting for the safety of the Republic.

Even before the opening shots had disturbed the calm of the Charleston harbor in April, 1861, it had been clear that diplomacy would play a weighty part in the efforts of Southern states to dissolve the Union. Henry's father, Charles Francis Adams, had been dispatched to London to foil the Southern quest for international aid. He knew that the European powers had the strength to intervene decisively should they wish to. The mere recognition of the Confederacy's independence would open to it the resources of armaments, supplies, and money to resist indefinitely. This had been the calculation of the radicals who rushed the South toward secession. In their blindness, they imagined that they held in their grasp the one precious commodity that would turn all the world to their will. Cotton was king, they proclaimed, and for its possession the great manufacturing nations of the Old World would rush to curry favor with the Confederacy.

The Southern statesmen whose hopes ran in this vein were not long in being sadly disabused. It was true, after a year or so of war, Britain began to suffer from a cotton famine, and the factories of Birmingham and Manchester slowed the pace of their production. In France too the want of the precious staple created a minor economic crisis. But it was not over the question of cotton that Europeans were divided in their attitude towards the American war. Rather, they took sides, because they perceived that the war involved the whole future of the Republic and of the way of life it represented.

A fundamental proposition was being tested: could a great nation survive and expand with its government in the hands of common people, or must it inevitably revert to some form of aristocracy? This was the question involved in the future of slavery or freedom in America. This was also the question bound up in Lincoln's denial that a state could secede and, of its own accord, destroy the government established by the people of the United States. The task of the Adamses, father and son, was to make that question clear to the English.

In some sectors of English society, the North found immediate sympathizers among men who understood the relationship of the war to the cause of liberty. One of them was John Bright, a Quaker and man of peace. A few years before he had spoken out boldly against the Crimean War. But in the American Civil War he saw other issues that held him to the Union side. In the half century of his life, England had advanced with gigantic steps towards the modernity of mass production. Bright was not tired of change; rather he resented its slowness. He longed for improvements in political and social legislation equivalent to those taking place in technology. In the way were an outmoded

aristocracy and a monarchy that had resolutely opposed every step away from the past. But America
seemed to offer the opportunities denied by Britain.
For America in its marvelous growth in every sphere
was the living demonstration of what men could
achieve without the cumbersome burden of worn-out
institutions.

A square-shaped man who customarily turned up in
the House of Commons in plain dress, Bright was
through and through a liberal, a democrat, and a republican. As a member of Parliament from the indus-
trial city of Birmingham, it required considerable
political courage and integrity on his part to argue for
the cause of the Union, regardless of the sacrifices that
support of the North might entail for the profits of the
textile companies and the wages of the millworkers,
on whose votes he was dependent. With him stood a
large body of opinion in England, in France, and
throughout the Continent. Yes, even the cotton-mill
workers thrown out of employment by the War re-
sponded to Bright's leadership, moved by a vision of
their own larger interests.

Numerous as they were, such men as Bright, Richard
Cobden, and William E. Forster were not in power in
1861. For thirteen years the conservatives of the Continent had been in the ascendancy. The revolutions of
1848 had threatened to destroy the older order. In
desperation, the ancient regime had closed ranks and
struck back. The shattered nobility had reformed and

accepted an alliance with the men of new wealth. The established churches and the monarchs, shaky from the fleeting nightmare of a throneless Europe, had joined the alliance which was now everywhere dominant. The Hapsburg Emperor, the Romanoff Czar, the Hohenzollern King of Prussia, stifled the Continent in reaction — shrewder and more flexible than in the past, but nonetheless determined to resist the newness of which the United States was the symbol.

Of the alliance of reaction, the Emperor of France was the leading spokesman. Louis Napoleon Bonaparte had come a long way since those early days when he had shivered in the fields, fighting with the Italian revolutionaries of 1831. He had gained a throne and lost his honor. A petty man, he had discovered in 1848 which was the winning side; and betraying his comrades in arms, he had pulled himself to power by a succession of coups. His uncle's great image he held constantly before him, yet he lacked the first Napoleon's daring and resolution.

Not infrequently Napoleon III was seized by the turncoat's fear of having chosen the wrong cause. Lurking memories of discarded hopes from time to time moved him to ruthless repression of the remnants of French liberalism. His secret police were active — even in the United States, where his spies kept watch over the agitation of radical refugees and labor leaders. For Louis Napoleon had disturbing recollections of the New World. He had crossed the Atlantic as a fugitive, and with his own eyes he had seen the growing power of the young Republic, and the vigorous spirit that attached its people to democracy. Better than any of the other crowned heads of Europe, he understood the menace of Americanism to the old order.

Incessant fright of the future also drove Napoleon III to seek security in a dynastic marriage. Fearful lest power be snatched from him, he imagined that he could plant his roots back in an imperial past by marrying a princess from one of the oldest lines in Europe, even if but from an obscure branch of it. After 1853 a queen of Spanish origin reigned by his side in the palace of the Tuileries.

Eugénie de Montijo was the last blossom of the court of Madrid. For a century that court had been the scandal of Europe — thoroughly selfish, completely immoral, and dedicated to no larger interest than gratification of the whims of the royal family and its courtiers. Even now rumor linked the Queen of Spain in a love affair with a wandering pianist. This was the atmosphere in which Eugénie had grown up, vain and selfish, carefully guarding her honor, which was the price of a good marriage, and credulous to the point of superstition. In Paris, she imagined that she was surrounded by enemies of all sorts, and embarked, in the time-honored tradition of her house, upon a career of intrigue. Of the Americans and all they represented, she disapproved in any case; but in addition family reasons made her hostile to the Republic.

It was inevitable that Louis Napoleon and Eugénie should cook up an extravagant scheme for restraining republicanism even in the New World. They had taken under their wing a simple young Austrian archduke, whom they had singled out as Emperor of Mexico. The venture was not only intended to create an empire in the New World; it would also aid French business interests and sustain the Catholic Church, then under attack in Mexico. Unfortunately, no statesman in the government in Paris had ability or courage enough to point out the disastrous flaws in the plan.

Reassured by promises of French support, with an entourage and an army supplied by Louis Napoleon, Maximilian in 1863 assumed the crown and prepared to go in person to govern his new domain. He had the support of the local conservative political clique in Mexico City. But most of his subjects were violently hostile. Imperial authority did not extend beyond the limits of the capital and the provinces were torn by full-scale revolts. Furthermore it was altogether clear that the United States would not recognize him; and, while the Republic was for the time being in tumult at home, it promised to give him its attention the moment that its domestic distractions ended. For Napoleon and Eugénie the potential threat from the North to the empire was an additional motive for desiring the failure of the

Union forces and the permanent division of the United States.

From the first, therefore, France was ready to aid the South. But it was not free to act without the agreement of England. Napoleon had too many irons in the fire to embroil himself in overseas commitments without the assurance that the British Navy would be friendly. The whole issue, therefore, turned on the attitude of the British Government.

In England a substantial body of conservative opinion favored the South and disunity. Tories who had not forgotten 1776 viewed with joy the collapse of the American experiment. Others considered the United States the source of the insidious republicanism and democracy that now threatened their own society. "The vaunted democracy," sneered *Blackwood's,* dragged from "his proper obscurity an ex-rail-splitter" and put "its liberties at his august disposal." Under British institutions, the magazine boasted, neither he nor any of his cabinet could have emerged "from the mediocrity to which nature had condemned them, and from which pure democracy alone was capable of rescuing them." In the House of Commons and the House of Lords a majority favored the Confederacy, and waited only the strategic opportunity for expressing that preference.

The final decision, however, rested with Queen Victoria's ministers. Three members of the British cabinet were in a position to affect the critical decision. The first was Lord Palmerston, the Prime Minister, an old hand at politics, who was now in his seventies, and who could look back with satisfaction on an eventful career. All his life he had found it advantageous, and even amusing, to play the role of the wily diplomat, not bound by usual standards. Yet, in actuality, he had always been attentive to popular impulses; and, like his old master, Canning, he had taken the liberal side in foreign affairs and been friendly to the Americans.

With the two other most powerful members of the ministry, Palmerston had frequent fallings out. At the head of the Foreign Office stood Earl Russell, who was now approaching seventy. The noble earl was known to Americans as a liberal, for his name was associated with the great reform measures of the 1830's and 1840's. Yet he had no real taste for the role into which he had been forced by the exigencies of party politics. Time and again he found himself on the popular side, against his will. The Foreign Secretary was perfectly willing to recognize the South, and in December, 1861, had composed an ultimatum which, had it been dispatched, might well have led to war with the United States. Cooler heads had averted the crisis, but Russell continued to believe that the Union divided would make Britain stronger everywhere in North America. Such an outcome would free Canada from the threat of the expanding Yankees and would increase commercial opportunities in the South and in the North. Both regions would be dependent on England, which could then play one off against the other.

William Gladstone's calculations led to the same conclusion. But this man followed a more devious route. Gladstone's was a paradoxical nature, idealistic yet prone to actions which in others would have seemed unscrupulous compromises. The key to the paradox was his deep commitment to moral principles so lofty that they were altogether beyond the reach of practical politics. Since Gladstone was also swayed by the politician's will to get on, he had arrived through years of hard maneuvering at the comfortable technique of action by expediency and justification by principle. The technique worked because his brilliant mind could shape principle to the necessities of any occasion. Gladstone never outlived the conservatism that had once led him to proclaim himself "an out-and-out inequalitarian." This devout believer in an established crown, church, and aristocracy disliked the United States and was an earnest sympathizer with the South.

Palmerston, Russell, and Gladstone held the fate of the Union in their hands, and little did young Henry Adams, speculating on their motives, imagine that it was the first who was his friend, and the others who were his foes. For the moment the British cabinet hung back; it hesitated to take steps that would outrage liberal opinion at home. Furthermore, Charles

Francis Adams had let the English know in no uncertain terms that the United States would bitterly resent any expression of sympathy in behalf of the Confederacy.

Through the first year of the War, therefore, Her Majesty's Government was cautious. It recognized Southern belligerency, but not its national independence. It gave no official, direct support to the rebels, yet it permitted their agents to operate openly in the British Isles.

The crisis approached as 1862 drew to a close. Union defeats in the Peninsular Campaign and the Second Battle of Bull Run had only partially been offset by the victory at Antietam. There seemed no reason to expect that the South would ever be crushed. In October, at Newcastle, Gladstone openly announced that Jefferson Davis had made a nation.

But Palmerston's deliberateness held the English back. He would not be hastened by colleagues he disliked and distrusted. Yet, by January, 1863, another Union defeat at Fredericksburg had brought the point of intervention closer. Napoleon III, emboldened, proposed mediation and was rebuffed by the United States. He now awaited the nod of assent from London to proceed to more active steps on behalf of the Confederacy, which, for its part, had indicated it would support the Mexican empire.

In Britain a motion to force recognition in the House of Lords had failed through the ineptitude of its sponsors. Confederate sentiment had not, however, been shifted. In the House of Commons at the end of May, Southern sympathizers gave notice they would move that the government negotiate with the European powers to recognize the Confederacy. Through the month of June the friends of the Confederacy in Parliament, Roebuck and his collaborators, only waited for a propitious occasion before pushing the cabinet to action.

Meanwhile, in the shipyards, the Lairds were building a pair of rams and a cruiser to join the *Alabama* and the *Florida,* which were already at sea, creating havoc in the American merchant and whaling fleets. (Two hundred and fifty Yankee ships were to go to the bottom under their guns.) Charles Francis Adams had protested that the rams were warships, and ought not to be transferred to the Confederacy. Yet, shrewd men in London and Richmond had no doubt that somehow the ships would find themselves under the Stars and Bars and under the command of Confederate captains. In any case, a loan successfully floated by the Confederacy had just then yielded the means for paying for these ships and other supplies.

As London moved into the summer season described by Henry Adams, the time was ripe for a final effort to assure English recognition of the Confederacy. Support would then snowball in the other capitals of Europe, and the North would realize that reconquest was hopeless. Lincoln would at last accept the inevitable peace that would leave the South independent, and the United States permanently divided. These were the calculations of the statesmen in Richmond. Vice-President Alexander H. Stephens of the Confederacy, an old friend of Lincoln's, was even then preparing to negotiate the terms of such a peace.

It was only necessary, through some dramatic demonstration, to show the North the futility of further fighting and at the same time to demonstrate to Europe that the South could not be conquered. To that objective the best military minds of the Confederacy were turned.

On the surface of things two years of fighting had hardly changed the situation of 1861. The Confederacy had successfully beaten off the attacks upon its capital. It had suffered losses in the West, but these had not affected its center of power. Even in the remote regions of the South, the Confederacy could still strike back; only recently it had retaken Galveston from the Yankees. Secure on the defensive, the Confederacy had no doubt that it could resist indefinitely.

This defensive posture, however, was irksome to those who shaped the military policy of the South. President Jefferson Davis longed for the decisive moment that would establish the permanence of the Confederacy. He wished to be finished with the burdensome expenses of war, and free to lead the new nation toward the romantic destiny he envisioned for it. In

Richmond he moved through the laborious tasks of his office, impatient with the necessity that compelled his government to waste its substance on war. If only the energies of the new state were not squandered before then, peace brought by some single decisive blow would justify secession.

This also was the desire of the Commander in Chief of the Army of Virginia. Ever since he had resigned his commission in the Army of the United States to take command of the Confederate forces, Robert E. Lee had remained on the defensive. On the familiar ground of Northern Virginia he had brilliantly frustrated the successive Union stabs at Richmond. But he was weary of being attacked, weary of seeing the battle rage back and forth across the lovely landscape he cherished. He knew what the war was costing his people; and he knew also that there would be no end to it in this interminable, bloody beating off of one thrust after another from the North.

In any case, it was not thus that he saw himself, ever parrying, ever waiting for the enemy, and with no power of initiative. He had preferred that other war in Mexico, in 1846 — a war of long marches and daring assaults. An inner image of himself flickered frequently in his thoughts — the vision of a gallant leader riding forward. No doubt it was that vision which, at a review on June 8, led him impulsively to put his horse, Traveller, at a gallop, to ride wildly three miles forward and three miles back.

What Lee wanted was some decisive feat that would bring a satisfying peace to the South. Again and again his mind came back to a daring idea. As the spring of 1863 drew to a close, his resolution was fixed. Determined to believe in its success, he minimized the risks involved and persuaded himself and the government that his strategy was feasible.

The problem before him, he thought, "resolved itself into a choice of one of two things — either to retire to Richmond and stand a siege, which must ultimately have ended in surrender, or to invade Pennsylvania." Of the two he preferred the latter. He would abandon the defensive and strike boldly at the heart of the North. It would not be difficult to confuse the Union Army at a time when it was still leaderless. McClellan was discredited. Lee could sweep to the left of the mountains directly toward the interior of Pennsylvania. Only forty miles away, waiting to be taken, was Harrisburg, the capital of Pennsylvania.

From the strictly military point of view, the strategic utility of the move was questionable. This region was not vital to the economy of the North; and the attack might not seriously disturb the Union armies. But the psychological value of the plan was incalculable. Northern morale, already shaken by heavy drafts of men and by the financial sacrifices of the war, would collapse. The Democratic governors of the Northern states would be bolstered in their growing discontent with Republican administration. Dissension would spread. The Yankees would at last perceive the futility of continuing the long struggle. Most important of all, the seizure of the capital of one of the great Northern states — not guarded as Washington was — would be the convincing demonstration to friends of the South throughout Europe that the Confederacy was unbeatable. Such a stroke would in short order earn the recognition so eagerly desired.

On June 3, General Lee began to move his splendid force toward the Shenandoah Valley. The Union Army, uncertain of his intentions, took up a dilatory pursuit.

Following the line of the Shenandoah, Lee moved slowly northward, keeping the mountains between him and the Federal troops. At the middle of the month he crossed the Potomac, and by the twenty-third his advance forces were in Pennsylvania, approaching Chambersburg in the Cumberland Valley.

At this juncture Lee suffered his first loss, although he would not for two weeks realize its importance. He sent the main body of his cavalry, under J. E. B. Stuart, off on one of its sweeping raids through Maryland. Finding the road to Washington almost open, Stuart was tempted to approach to within four miles of the Federal capital. In that act of useless daring, he was separated from Lee's main army. Union troops moved in between the two Southern forces and prevented

Stuart from rejoining his chief. Deprived of his cavalry, Lee thereafter acted without precise knowledge of where the enemy stood and in what numbers.

Meanwhile, the whole of Lee's army had marched into Pennsylvania, and his advance force was now only twenty miles from Harrisburg. By the end of June the Confederates were within ten miles of the Pennsylvania capital.

Lee prepared for the decisive battle. He could not advance further north for, without his cavalry, he had no idea of the whereabouts of the Union Army. From a spy behind the Yankee lines, he learned that the Federals under a new commander, Meade, had crossed the Potomac after him. But, he confessed, "I do not know what to do without General Stuart, the eye of the army." Undecided, he therefore pitched camp along the eastern slope of South Mountain near Cashtown, and, with his rear protected, waited for the opportunity to resume his advance.

There he seemed likely to stay, because the Union Army was not in a position to launch an aggressive attack. It had just suffered one of its periodic changes of command, as George Gordon Meade replaced Fighting Joe Hooker. Meade was a man of extravagant caution — as the next week would prove. He had no intention of leading his army into an attack that might be as disastrous as those that had overwhelmed his predecessors in the command. He took a position behind Pike Creek in Maryland and waited for Lee to attack him. On the last day of June, 1863, the two armies rested in the lovely rolling countryside that would soon be stained by their blood.

Lee then had no fixed plan of operations, for Stuart's cavalry had still not rejoined him, and he was uncertain as to just where the Army of the Potomac would turn up. He had to choose between the alternatives of retreating back down the valley of the Cumberland and the Shenandoah or of advancing on to Harrisburg. Either course was risky in the absence of accurate information as to Meade's whereabouts. Of necessity he decided to stay where he was and to await the outcome of events.

Then a chance encounter precipitated the decisive battle that neither Lee nor Meade was seeking. Advancing into enemy territory, the Confederate commanders had looked with envy upon the pleasant towns as yet untouched by war. The neat homes and well-stocked shops offered a poignant contrast with the country they had left behind. For the soldiery it was worse. Ill-equipped and short of supplies, they had come into a region abounding in goods of every sort. On the 28th, Lieutenant General Early had laid the town of York under the tribute of cash and shoes. Elsewhere marching soldiers snatched the hats from off the heads of civilian bystanders to shield themselves from the hot June sun. Now, as they waited, momentarily idle, they thought of fitting themselves out even better.

Ten miles from the Confederate encampment was

the thriving town of Gettysburg, a regional market center. On June 30, part of General A. P. Hill's division drifted down to see whether they could replenish their stock of boots there. Marching alertly on the hot summer roads they approached the Lutheran seminary on a hill just west of the little town. There, by surprise, they came upon the advance guard of the Army of the Potomac, Buford's cavalry division. So began the four-day battle that would, in a longer perspective, determine the fate of the Confederacy and the Union.

Drawn into the conflict unexpectedly, each commander committed himself slowly to the decisive struggle. On July first the Confederates drove the Union forces through the town of Gettysburg and southward into the open fields. There the two forces took positions on opposing ridges that commanded the main road back to the South. Their names would acquire heart-rending familiarity in the memories of survivors and of the kin of those who died there — Seminary Ridge where Lee rested, and Cemetery Ridge where Meade drew the Federal forces together.

At this point Lee took the offensive. He did so against the strong opposition of his senior corps commander, Longstreet. But Lee knew that he could no longer afford to wait. He could only attack or withdraw; and to withdraw was to abandon all hope for the dramatic blow that would bring peace out of an interminable war. The only chance lay in a desperate attack, at whatever odds and against whatever difficulties.

On July 2 came the first of the great lunges against the entrenched Union defenses. This was an unco-ordinated movement aimed at the flanks of the Union line. The Southerners advanced, in the north, up the slopes of Culp's Hill; in the south, through the Peach Orchard and across the rocks of the Devil's Den. For a brief hour Lee's men held the heights, then they were driven back by Federal reinforcements.

On July 3 came the second, climactic, assault. An indecisive struggle at the southern end of the ridge occupied the morning; then it subsided, and quiet fell across the torn battlefield. Thirty thousand casualties had already been carried away. In his headquarters northwest of the battlefield Lee with increasing desperation pondered the alternatives of advance and retreat. His hopes mounted with each onward surge; and he refused to let them fall with each withdrawal that followed.

Already Lee had determined that if he could not turn his enemy's flanks, he would stake all in a daring thrust at the very heart of the Union position. In the quiet hour, as noon passed, he prepared to throw fifteen thousand men against Cemetery Ridge in a supreme effort to break through and destroy Meade's army. Longstreet, knowing the desperate odds against them, argued to the point of insubordination for a retreat. But the gray man on the gray horse would not surrender his dream of victory.

Thus across the torn fields the men advanced, in the

long lines of a charge, the bright banners dotting the green fields with color. They came fiercely, the sword-waving officers — some of them mounted — in the lead. They advanced, eager and confident, spurred on by the rebel yell of the Old South that was to die with them that afternoon.

They had gone halfway across the fields, some 250 yards, and still had met no opposition. Then, as they crossed the Emmitsburg Road and approached the slopes of the Ridge, the Union artillery opened a murderous fire on them. A fence and beyond it a stone wall halted the Confederates just long enough to frame them as a perfect target for the Yankee marksmen. Yet the suicidal attack continued, carrying a few survivors to the very crest of the Ridge. But the decimated group who made it found the ground impossible to hold. The Union troops closed in about them, and the handful who had stormed the Ridge were shot down or captured. The main Confederate force retreated back up to its base. In the brief engagement twenty-seven generals had fallen and thousands of their men.

Lee had come forward to the line of battle and met the retreating remnants of his shattered divisions. "This has been my fight," he told General Pickett, who led the charge, "and upon my shoulders rests the blame." The commander readied his men for the counterattack that did not come, and took stock once more of the situation.

On July 4, Lee was still in position weighing the possibilities for a further attack. Then at last he faced up to what he had not wished to see: he had no hope of winning. That evening Lee yielded to the facts. Somberly, in the dark, the great army gave up its hope for victory and peace, and retreated south to the Potomac. The dream of conquest had ended.

Many dreams died that day on the bloody fields of Gettysburg. The little cemetery on the hill, grown large now, had been consecrated by the brave men who struggled there. From every end of the country, from many parts of the world they had converged upon this Pennsylvania hill to bury there the delusion that secession might succeed. And in that burial they had determined that government of the people, by the people, for the people should not perish from the earth. The South fought on for want of alternative, but no longer in the conviction that it could win. It was thereafter a matter of time before the greater strength of the North crushed the last embers of hope for the Confederacy.

For it was now clear that aid from Europe would not come. The news of the battle went back to London, where the Adams family received it with jubilation. Henry got the word on Sunday afternoon, on the way to a small reception at the home of his friend Monckton Milnes. When Milnes heard the news, "with a whoop of triumph" he threw both arms about Henry and kissed him "on both cheeks."

The British cabinet now knew it could not intervene, and accepted the prospect of an ultimate Union
victory. Across the channel, Napoleon III also grasped
the significance of the event, and surrendered his hopes
of an empire in the New World. Maximilian's flimsy
empire survived a few years more, until American
pressure and Mexican revolutionaries ended it against
a stone wall, before a firing squad.

And with these dreams also died the last hopes of
European reactionaries that the American experiment
in democratic republicanism would fail. The victory of
Gettysburg was assurance that the Republic would
survive and the Union be maintained.

In 1867, as the English approached a democratic
franchise, in 1871 as the Parisian revolutionaries
pulled apart Napoleon's empire, the European consequences of the demonstration became apparent. Men
struggling for their own freedom could not then be mis-
guided by the argument that democracy had failed in
America.

At home, the Union, now one and indivisible from
coast to coast, has never again faced the question as to
its identity or authority. These were the stakes of the
momentous struggle that swayed across the fields of
Gettysburg.

CHAPTER FIVE

Mr. Seward's Bargain

ALWAYS the Americans had been fond of looking ahead to a grandiose future. The history of their development as a people had incessantly fed their faith in progress; and progress they identified with their own continued growth. The unconditional surrender of the South in 1865 dispelled the threat of disunity, and the aspiration of the veterans lately returned from war looked ahead to the prospect of a constantly expanding destiny. They differed only as to the form and direction they supposed that expansion would take.

Few, however, attached their hopes to the continent's northernmost extremity. Those little known, desolate spaces, lost beneath the snow of almost continuous winter, seemed doomed to perpetual emptiness. Little had come of the Russian attempts to plant settlements there. And indeed, no sober statesman, reckoning the balance of possibilities, could foresee the future wealth of Alaska — the outpouring of gold and oil, of furs and fish, of gas, timber, pulp, and tin with which it was ultimately to enrich the nation.

No more could such a man have guessed at the immense strategic significance of this corner of the North Pacific. True enough, the visionary de Tocqueville had once predicted that the United States would someday face the Russian empire in opposition. But to the Americans who noted it, that prophetic observation referred only to the rivalry between their system of government and the Czarist despotism. No one, of course, conceived that a shift of interests in the Pacific and a new geography of flight would give this region crucial value at a moment when the United States was locked in massive competition with Russia, with the outcome certain to determine the fate of the whole world. No one therefore was then concerned about what the disposition of power might be were Russia established in North America, only four hundred miles away from the borders of the United States.

That Russia did not remain fixed there was due to a series of unrelated incidents — the death of an anxious lover, a humiliating defeat on the fields of Crimea, and the decay of a great Asian empire — to these, and to the determination of an aging statesman who valued a neglected corner of the continent for the wrong reasons.

The momentous consequences of the transfer of Alaska to American hands were by no means foreseen or understood when the Czar's government agreed to it. For the Russians, as for all Europeans whose minds had earlier turned to it, this was mostly a land of abandoned dreams.

Alaska and the Arctic North had been a graveyard for hopes for more than three hundred years so far. Nothing good had ever come of them. The hopes had risen with the discovery of the new continent. Men whose expectations of fortune were fixed on trade with the gilded East of Cathay and the Indies refused to believe that America altogether blocked them off. As the daring ships probed the long Atlantic coastline and revealed its unbroken extent from south to north, the conviction took hold that somewhere in the Northwest was a passage, from sea to sea and onward to the East.

With the southern oceans closed off to them, a gallant company of Englishmen had beaten vainly against the Arctic wastes in search of the Northwest Passage. Here Hudson's fragile vessel had nosed into the great bay that was to bear his name; and afterwards for more than a century successive expeditions had poked persistently through the ponderous floes in the quest for a sea road leading to the East.

The mariners and those who invested in their expeditions fed their hopes from a fund of apocryphal stories about these regions. Geography in the eighteenth century still consisted largely of a body of approximate guesses, among which it was hard to distinguish the mythical from the real. Trusted maps in all honesty for years located the nonexistent Straits of Anian at the entrance to the presumed Northwest Passage; and

many a shrewd seaman accepted at face value the tales
of discoveries ascribed to Juan de Fuca, to Maldonado,
and to Admiral de Fonte — all garbled products of in-
ventive imaginations.

According to popular belief these discoveries had
brought the Pacific opening of the great strait within
reach. The excited calculations of statesmen and ex-
plorers turned upon the means of gaining control of
the golden route.

In 1776, the British Admiralty Commissioners determined to find the water passage from the Pacific to
Hudson's Bay. Twenty thousand pounds were held out
as a prize for the fortunate discoverer, and on its own
account the Admiralty sent forth Captain James Cook
to try to trace the western coast of America north of
latitude 65°.

Cook set off on the voyage from which he was never
to return. It took him almost two years to circle the
Cape of Good Hope, pass through the Southern Pacific,
and, after discovering the Hawaiian Islands, to move
north to the forbidding coast that he was instructed to
explore. Looking carefully into every likely inlet, he
painfully made his way to above the Arctic Circle,
where he was halted by the solid walls of floating ice
at latitude 70°. Fearful of the approaching winter, he
then withdrew to Hawaii to prepare for another venture in the following spring.

Cook never again saw the white Arctic barrier. A
minor skirmish with the Hawaiian natives cost him his

life, and the expedition was forced to go back to the north without him in the summer of 1779. His tired seamen pushed the two battered sloops toward the old goal with no better fortune than before and, finally weary of the effort, turned back to England.

Such expeditions had been dispatched in the face of the stubborn Spanish claim to all of western America. But foreign activity in the area at last aroused the Spaniards to the necessity of making good the title given them, almost three centuries before, by the Papal line of demarcation. In the 1760's they had taken the first steps toward establishing posts on the California coast at San Diego and Monterey. In the 1770's, their ships had come well north of the Columbia River; and in 1788 an expedition under Estevan José Martinez had set out to clear interlopers off the coast. At Nootka Sound (Vancouver Island), in May, 1789, Martinez encountered a group of English traders. Frenchmen and Americans were also active in the vicinity, he learned. But most serious of all were the signs of the steady advance of the Russians.

While the conquistadors and the seadogs of England had led the thrust of European expansion westward, the subjects of the Muscovite Czar had been moving laboriously eastward across the vast dark spaces of Siberia. Much the same sort of restless spirits had been involved in the two movements — adventurers incapable of falling into a settled life, merchants driven by the quest for new wealth, men of violence, the discontented and the rebellious.

In the 1580's Yermak Timofeiev, a Cossack fleeing the consequences of his brigandage, pushed across the Ural Mountains and defeated the Tartars. Some fifty years later, the Russians had edged across the half-empty plains of Siberia to the Pacific at Okhotsk. Among the nomadic tribes, white traders and hunters and an occasional retinue of tax collectors insinuated themselves. In the 1720's, Peter the Great occasionally turned his attention to the unexploited empire in the east, and it was he who set on foot the plans to extend it to America.

At this time no one yet knew whether America was joined to Asia or not. Vitus Bering, a Dane in the service of Peter's new navy, was directed to find out. His actions showed a daring willingness to take risks and yet withal a capacity for attention to detail that others sometimes construed as excessive caution. Offended pride once led him to give up his commission; yet the challenge of his task was to lead him on for seventeen years in the service of capricious and unsympathetic masters.

His mission was no less than this: to cover the six thousand miles from St. Petersburg to farthest Siberia, taking with him the necessary supplies to build his ships at the ocean's edge and then to map the uncharted seas beyond.

He left the Russian capital on his first journey in

February, 1725; and three and a half years later, having built his own ships at the mouth of the Kamchatka River, he traced the northern outlines of the eastern Asiatic coast. At latitude 67° North, he satisfied himself that America and Asia were not connected, and turned back out of fear of the threatening ice floes. Returning to St. Petersburg he persuaded the government to sponsor a second exploration. He set off again in February, 1734, at the head of a far more elaborate expedition. More than seven years of strenuous preparation and struggle with recalcitrant Czarist officials followed before his ships at last set sail from Avacha Bay in Siberia in June, 1741. This time his course was directly eastward, and before his death, on an unknown island, he had charted the Aleutians and the Gulf of Alaska and made the whole area Russian.

Nothing happened thereafter for a half-century. The expense of Bering's expeditions soured Peter the Great's successors on further Arctic adventures. Besides, they were more concerned with the wars in Europe in which they pushed forward Russia's frontiers toward the Baltic and the Black seas. The American extremity of the empire was left largely to itself. Onto the Aleutians there drifted a motley crew of frontiersmen. Siberian merchants, tough-living men whose operations extended over two continents, from the fairs of the homeland to the markets of China, were not slow to estimate the fur resources of the new lands. In the van were the hunters, sometimes agents on their own account, sometimes acting for the merchants. The *promyshlenniki,* as they were called, left the forests and took to the sea. In the rude boats they built with their own hands they descended upon the Red Indian settlements, seized the women, drove the men out to hunt for pelts, and, when they were ready, made off with the bundled wealth in skins. Now and again the outraged Aleuts revolted; then for a time red man and white outdid each other in cruel massacres, until the superiority of the gun made itself felt decisively.

It was to such masters as these that Alaska had been abandoned by the time Cook sailed northward from Hawaii. But the English expedition was to alter the fortunes of the Russian outpost.

Cook's men, sailing dejectedly homeward, had stopped off at Canton. In the Chinese metropolis they discovered an amazing market for what they had hitherto little valued — their cargo of furs, sea otter and seal, picked up from the *promyshlenniki* up north. The fabulous prices tempted the crew to return to the frozen waters from which it had so recently escaped. Only naval discipline kept them on the course toward England.

The news, however, spread around the world. It drew Captain Gray in the *Columbia* to the river that bears the name of his ship, and led him to pioneer the American China trade. In Russia, it prompted ambitious merchants to explore the possibilities of establishing a more permanent and more extensive occupation of America. Were the territory to be exploited efficiently, the new Chinese markets for fur promised extravagant returns.

Three men, in particular, evolved the plan for its exploitation. Had these succeeded, Alaska might today be Russian.

The first of them, Grigori Ivanovich Shelekhov, was a merchant, a man of considerable wealth who in later life had his portrait painted in the French fashion, wearing a stylish coat with lace at his cuffs and at his throat, and a ribboned decoration stuck prominently on his chest. Yet, beneath the powdered wig, shrewd brutal eyes still stared boldly forth from the canvas, and told more of his character than the graceful pose in which the artist had set him.

Shelekhov had come east from Russia to Okhotsk in 1776, and had there taken up the strenuous life of a fur trader. He differed from the rest of his competitors in the driving ambition that left him discontented with any but the highest prizes. Artful and determined, he pushed ahead. In a half-dozen years he had formed his own company and was ready to launch the most hazardous enterprise of his career.

His first and immediate design was to plant a colony in America that would become the central receiving station for the whole fur trade. To this end he fitted out a small armada of three ships, and in 1783 led it himself to Kodiak Island, taking along his wife, Natalia Alexeyevna, the first white woman to sail these seas. In

a short time a settlement had sprung up at Three
Saints Bay. But beyond this, Shelekhov had a long-
range plan which was more extensive. He dreamed of
establishing a mammoth company, chartered by the
Crown, like the British East India Company, that
would absorb all competitors and through its monopoly
create a personal commercial empire. Once the Kodiak
colony was established on a firm footing, he hastened
back to St. Petersburg to win acceptance for his scheme
in the unfamiliar atmosphere of the imperial court.

The colony he left in the hands of Aleksandr Baranov,
a man endowed with every quality conducive to success
but one. Skill in calculation, determination, and courage,
he possessed in abundance; he lacked only the driving
will to disregard human factors, to crush his opponents,
to pounce on opportunity. Too often he was ready to
compromise, to accommodate those who needed his
aid, to trust his friends. When he, too, had his portrait
painted, he allowed himself to wear one decoration
for the occasion; but his hand held a quilled pen, not a
sword. That was a token of the difference between him
and Shelekhov.

Baranov's life had been a succession of misfortunes
until his path crossed that of Shelekhov. Baranov too
had been a merchant; but dishonest employees had
plundered his warehouses, careless ones had allowed
his glass factory to fall to pieces, and a rascally partner
had made off with his fortune. He was at his wits' end,
facing bankruptcy, in 1790 when Shelekhov offered

him the post of general manager of the Kodiak colony. Baranov accepted his lot, although he hated the distant wastes of the East, and was ever uncomfortable among the rough, tough men — both red and white — who were to be his companions for the rest of his life.

The new manager had no faith in the cold world which he now entered; he never shared the dreams of a commercial empire in the Pacific that moved his master. But he was a superb administrator. His task was to keep the colony going and to gather pelts, and for that he was eminently qualified. Within a few years, he had organized the Aleuts into a remarkable fur-gathering apparatus capable of sending forth in quest of sea otters as many as five hundred seagoing *baidarkas* — that indestructible three-man craft, like the smaller kayak of the Eskimo, which is capable of moving through any waters. Within ten years Baranov moved the American headquarters of the company forward to Sitka on the Alaska mainland, and shortly thereafter he was able to plant a thriving outpost at Fort Ross in California.

Meanwhile, in St. Petersburg, Shelekhov was less successful in his quest for a company charter. In court circles he met endless evasion; there seemed to be no way of breaking through to a decision. He took each pretext for refusal seriously, and wore himself out in the composition of laborious memoranda demonstrating that his proposal was in the interests of the Empress, of her subjects, and of the Orthodox faith. He died in 1795, having failed to secure the coveted charter.

Yet, in the Russian capital, Shelekhov had attained one aim that would ultimately bring his great dream within a hair's breadth of realization. Earlier his social ambitions had led him to choose a wife from among the country gentry. Now they drove him to seek his daughter's husband among the nobility. A year before his death, he had married his Anne Grigorievna to Nikolai Petrovich Rezanov.

Rezanov was the scion of a noble family from the province of Smolensk. A member of the new generation, brought up under the pervasive influence of the ideas of the French Enlightenment with their idealization of Nature, he had become imbued with the romance of striving against the wilderness. He was a minor official in Catherine the Great's court when he met his future wife and her father; and no doubt the old man's golden visions attracted him as much as the beauty of the daughter. The new son-in-law made Shelekhov's ambitions his own, but in a grander form.

The company which Rezanov now envisaged would be a commercial empire stretching in an imperial semicircle around the entire northern Pacific, from the Kamchatka peninsula across to the Aleutians, from there to the Alaska coast and down to California, with perhaps a base in Hawaii. Permanent settlements of artisans and husbandmen would make the area self-sufficient, while carefully planned exploitation of its fur resources would give its rulers a dominant position in the China trade and a steady inflow of gold. Fired by this grandiose vision and more skilled than his father-in-law in the ways of the Palace, Rezanov was able to thread the mazes of the court circles, and finally at the very end of 1799 he secured the charter that created the Russian-American Company.

When Rezanov left Russia for the North Pacific in August, 1803, his hopes seemed well on their way to fulfillment. The young Czar, Alexander I, was of the same romantic generation as his own; and Rezanov had succeeded in gaining his ear in pleading the necessity of spreading Russian civilization to this remote corner of the earth.

And then, who was to stop them? All Europe was divided in war. Britain could spare no energies from the struggle with France; Napoleon had no ambitions here and was anxious to mollify the Russians; soon, in fact, he would meet Alexander at Tilsit to divide up the world between them. As for the Spaniards, they were divided by internal dissensions and could scarcely hold on to what they already had.

Even the sight of Sitka did not dishearten the courtier. Rezanov reached the little settlement in 1805, shortly after the Russians had beaten off the hostile Kolosh Indians. The squalor of the place was overwhelming, for the *promyshlenniki* and their Red Indian cohorts were not in normal times overly fastidious in their way of life, and the reek of decaying fish and furs being cured always shocked newcomers. Hard-pressed by recent fighting, the Russian settlers had neglected the buildings, which were in sad need of repair. Supplies had dwindled dangerously, scurvy was spreading, and the toll of deaths had begun to mount. It was soon apparent to Rezanov that the colony was doomed unless fresh supplies could be brought in to save it. And those supplies could be secured quickly only from the Spaniards in California. Knowing that such trade was forbidden by Spanish law, he nevertheless resolved to sail south and to make the essential effort himself.

In California, he found the mission friars willing enough to trade; they sympathized with the plight of the Russians and valued their furs. But the stubborn Spanish commandant of California, Argüello, was more difficult. He was courteous enough to the courtly Rezanov, treated him with respect, and lavished on him the best entertainment that the place afforded. But when it came to business, he stubbornly refused to wink at a violation of the law.

But the commandant had a daughter called Doña Concepción. She was a lonely young girl limited in this remote outpost both by the rigidities of Spanish eti-quette and by the absence of companionship. The noble young man from far away St. Petersburg soon won her heart, and she was unable to hide her true feeling for long. Cynically, Rezanov, already married, nevertheless seized the opportunity to exploit her emotions, in order to convince the father through the daughter. During the long delay on shore, he pressed his courtship vigorously and successfully. He won over Doña Concepción and her parents and the local clergy. And as a prospective son-in-law, he at last secured the coveted permission to trade. He returned to his own colony triumphant.

Now, however, Rezanov discovered that he was trapped by his own emotions. Originally, he had planned to leave Sitka at once to complete the commercial arrangements for the company's future operations. Already his itinerary was marked out; but somehow he found no pleasure in the thought of setting out to forge links of new trade in Manila, China, and India. He no longer had any heart for that journey.

Instead, his mind kept wandering back to California. He could not forget the lonely girl who waited joyously in the mission for his return. Concepción, who was to have been a mere tool in his hands, had now suddenly become the sole object of his desires. Brooding in his loneliness, he examined his conscience. Was the betrayal he had plotted worthy of him? Did it not make him one with the savages about him? Distaste for his callousness slowly mounted within him as he huddled dejectedly in his filthy, insect-infected quarters.

Then he made up his mind. He would keep his

promise. Like the heroes of his imagination, he would surmount every obstacle, forget all material considerations, to save his honor and his love. He determined to return immediately to St. Petersburg to secure the necessary imperial and ecclesiastical dispensations that would free him for a new marriage.

In haste he set out on the long voyage home, impatiently he crossed the sea, and at a forced pace he pushed himself across the great wilderness through the worst of the Siberian winter. At the back of his mind loomed up the gloomy realization that the Czar and the Church would not readily consent. But he downed those disturbing reflections in the single-minded fury with which he drove on his animals, his men, and himself.

At Krasnoyarsk, still a long way from his destination, he fell ill. His fevered mind and exhausted body proved unequal to their burdens, and early in 1807, he died.

Doña Concepción never saw her lover return. And thus Alaska never achieved the imperial destiny that Shelekhov and Rezanov had dreamed for it. Bereft of these two leaders, the company lost its driving spirit and sank into a lethargic and unaggressive prosperity. As manager, Baranov had no dreams for conquest. His competence was equal only to the maintenance from existing fur sales of a decent level of dividends to the company stockholders.

At that unimaginative level of operations, the colony survived under Baranov and his successors. Arrangements were made with American merchants and British fur companies whereby the strenuous trapping and trading functions were delegated to others in return for secure annual payments. Sitka and its outposts grew comfortable and staid; and when, in 1841, it seemed profitable to do so, Fort Ross in California was sold to John Sutter, the Swiss entrepreneur who was to achieve fame within the decade by his discovery of gold.

By this time too the Czars had lost interest. Alexander himself had long before diverted his interests to Europe, where he labored first in collaboration with Napoleon and then for the destruction of the French Empire. After Waterloo, he again thought briefly of his American possession. Absorbed by his mystical scheme of a Holy Alliance, Alexander intended to establish over the whole earth the reactionary peace of which he had become the prime mover ever since he had turned against Napoleon. For a while he imagined that he could sterilize the source of republican infection in the Western Hemisphere, and thus keep Europe safe from liberalism and democracy. He labored to keep the revolting colonies of Spain in the hands of the Bourbons; and a pretentious ukase closed the Northwest to all but the Russians. But the Monroe Doctrine and the hostility of Great Britain punctured those pretensions, and thereafter Alaska became only the outermost extremity of Russia's vast Siberian holdings, without much intrinsic interest or importance.

This peaceable stalemate in the Northern Pacific might have persisted indefinitely. No vital concerns were involved, and Russian suzerainty over these empty wastes seemed likely to go on undisturbed. Then, at midcentury, the repercussions of the momentous collapse of two ancient empires caused a new upheaval in Alaska.

The heyday of the Ottomans and the Manchus was now approaching its finish. Their long hegemony over a quarter of the earth's surface was ending. Weakened from within, neither was capable of maintaining itself against the mounting forces of assault from without. In eastern Europe and in eastern Asia, the ambitious states of the West were arraying themselves for the struggle to snatch up the pieces that would be left by the ultimate dismemberment of China and Turkey. And in both areas, Britain and Russia were the great rivals in the conflict that was to follow.

For more than a century the Czars had directed their energies in a drive toward the Balkans and the Black Sea. Now their advances towards Constantinople were a direct threat to the British. Were they to secure access to the Mediterranean, England's supremacy in this part of the world would be directly challenged. For almost forty years after Waterloo a series of parries and thrusts had occupied the statesmen of the two nations; and in 1854 the disastrous war in the Crimea had brought the issue out into the open.

Russia's defeat in this war led to a time of reckoning. The massive incompetence of the Czarist administration called for a succession of internal reforms, and military failure called for a reassessment of the strategic situation. On the first score the government was attracted by the liberal economic policies that had succeeded so remarkably in Britain. To some Russians in the court such monopolistic companies as the Russian American were relics of the past to be eliminated as quickly as possible. And strategically Alaska was in an exposed position, difficult to defend. During the war English sea power had dominated the Pacific. In any future conflict the British Navy could hardly be prevented from taking Alaska at will. Thus, in the 1850's, the question was increasingly debated in St. Petersburg, whether the American territory was worth keeping at all.

If it was to be held, it certainly needed strengthening; and the necessary resources could more profitably be expended elsewhere, argued Nikolai Muraviëv, governor general of eastern Siberia since 1847. Muraviëv had watched British expansion in southern China with envy, and had himself begun to encroach on Manchu territory with a series of bases in the Amur river valley. Why should his country's men and materials be diverted to the worthless spaces of North America, from which came only miserable bundles of fur, when they could be used to exploit the immense wealth of Korea and Manchuria and ultimately of all North China?

Muraviëv's arguments seemed unanswerable. Sometime before 1860 the Czar decided Alaska was not worth holding and might be sold to any power but England.

The events of the next five years made the Americans desirable purchasers from the Russian point of view. The Czar had no love for the Western Republic, nor any desire to strengthen or extend it. But Anglo-American tensions during the Civil War and the unsettled problems that continued to trouble the relations of Washington with London convinced him that the transfer of Alaska to the United States would weaken England or at least create an additional source of dissension. In 1865 the Russian Government had signified its willingness to sell Alaska to the United States.

It was by no means certain, however, that the United States was willing to buy. Earlier suggestions looking towards the acquisition of this northernmost region of the continent had evoked no enthusiasm in Washington. Many Americans saw no necessity for further expansion, while great areas of the country were still unsettled; and those who did thought that the proper direction of our growth was southeastward toward Cuba and the Caribbean. To almost everyone, Alaska seemed likely to be a useless encumbrance.

Only one statesman, nursing stale dreams as his career drew to a close, was convinced that Alaska was destined to be American.

William H. Seward had also been marked for assassination when Booth's bullet put an end to Lincoln's life; for the mad conspiracy had been directed at the Secretary of State as well as at the President. But Seward, wounded, had lived while Lincoln died.

At the war's end, Seward was almost sixty-five and knew his active political career had not much further to go. He had largely put aside his personal ambitions. The presidency, for which he felt he was far better qualified than Lincoln, was now beyond his grasp; new and younger politicians were crowding onto the scene and would give but small regard to his earlier achievements. In the conflict between President Johnson and the radical Republicans, principle led him to side with the Chief Executive — and that had cost him considerable public and party popularity. He would serve out his terms as Secretary of State until 1869, and then withdraw into retirement.

Yet Seward longed to leave behind him some enduring accomplishment that would fulfill the promises of his youthful career. As governor for New York for four years he had built up a growing following of admirers. In the Senate in the 1850's, he had been preeminently the spokesman for the moderate antislavery sentiment of the North. His doctrine of the higher law had set moral principle above the Constitution and had provided slogans for a whole generation, until the brighter figure of Lincoln had eclipsed him. Now Seward was most eager, before his term of public service closed, to redeem himself by furthering the national interest in some monumental fashion.

Back in the 1840's, Seward like other Americans had believed it was his country's manifest destiny to occupy the whole continent. The advantages of their system of government and social order were so clear, they thought, that people everywhere would rush to adopt them once the opportunity were presented them. Indeed, it was only the obstruction of corrupt and undemocratic governments that prevented them from doing so. When the opportunity presented itself, the United States would brush aside those regimes, and the people would voluntarily adhere to the Union. In due course the whole continent would become the United States of America.

After 1846 the doctrine of "manifest destiny" seemed to Seward to have become entangled in the slaveholders' conspiracy to extend the area of servitude southward. Now that that danger had been averted, it was once more possible to extend the boundaries of the country outward in the interests of human liberty. The power of Spain was deteriorating and would not persist for long in the Western Hemisphere. The French had withdrawn from Mexico. Only the British and the Russians remained.

The English would be a problem, the Secretary of State knew. There was no likelihood that they would voluntarily relinquish their hold on Canada or on Central America, and powerful forces in the United States were interested in maintaining the peace that had pre-vailed since the establishment of the Oregon boundary in 1846.

Yet Seward was convinced that the day would come when we would move north. In 1861 he had been will-ing to provoke war with England and Spain in the rash hope that the shock treatment of trouble abroad would draw the seceded states back into the Union and, per-haps, add Canada to it as well. After 1865, when it was no longer necessary to keep England neutral, the day of reckoning seemed closer than ever. Seward was too cautious now to provoke war, but he was at least willing to tolerate and encourage the mad schemes of the Irish-American Fenians, who plotted the invasion of Canada.

For Seward, then, Alaska had a critical importance it possessed for few others. Acquisition of that terri-tory would eliminate one more alien power from the continent, it would extend American holdings, and it would threaten Canada from the north. Alaska was worth buying because it would open the way to ex-pansion over the whole continent.

When the Russian ambassador returned from a visit to St. Petersburg in the early spring of 1867, the Secre-tary of State leaped at his suggestion that a sale might be made. The terms were quickly agreed upon, and the next year the ratification of the purchase was pushed through an apathetic Senate and a dubious House. The utmost political pressure and personal cajolery were necessary to get Congress to agree to the consummation of "Seward's folly."

Seward himself retired; and the new territory attracted little public attention thereafter. Even later, when discoveries of gold and iron more than repaid the cost of £200,000, Alaska excited only momentary interest among Americans, and then receded from their consciousness — taken for granted.

Yet, had this opportunity been passed by, the Russians might never have been dislodged. By the end of the century the whole situation had changed. The discovery of gold and other mineral resources suddenly gave the territory a new and unexpected value. Furthermore the Czar was now acquiring the means to defend it. For the construction of the trans-Siberian railroad, which was completed at the turn of the century narrowed the distance between St. Petersburg and the Pacific, and allowed the Russians to establish naval bases at Port Arthur and Vladivostok which soon became important centers of power in the area. Not many years after 1867 the Russians might have been far from willing to give up Alaska.

In that event, the bases that today flank the northern ocean would not have been American, pointing toward Asia, but Russian, pointing toward the United States. If our citizens, in the air age, still feel that distance from the potential enemy gives some security to their national borders, it is in no small measure due to Mr. Seward's bargain.

CHAPTER SIX

A Dispatch to Hong Kong

SPRING came to Washington in 1898, as a distraction. The afternoons lengthened, the dogwood and forsythia burst into bloom, and the winter haze disappeared from the air. The inviting sun shone through the open windows of the office buildings and drew the minds of men away from the files of papers on the desks.

There was no more passionate lover of nature in the capital city than the Assistant Secretary of the Navy. Yet, it was in no springtime mood of anticipation that Theodore Roosevelt watched the March days go by. Bitterly resentful, he considered the indecision of his government ruinous, and again and again chafed at lost opportunities. His own counsel had been persistently rejected and President McKinley was, he feared, "resolute to have peace at any price."

Roosevelt had the dismayed feeling that no one knew as well as he what the necessities of the crisis demanded. Sometimes he wondered whether the officials of his government were even aware that a crisis existed.

His own ideas were simple and consistent. He was nearing forty, already a success in both politics and literature. He had no thought, however, of allowing himself to rest upon his laurels. With determination and energy he pushed himself onward. Life was a struggle, in which the fittest survived; laxity and ease led to decadence while continuous effort alone made men and peoples strong. He had himself learned this when, as a frail, string-bean of a youth, he had exposed himself to the harsh life of the West and built himself up through a regime of hard exercise. Even now, in approaching middle age, he would not rest. And, in fiery words that were not altogether incongruous with his high, squeaky voice, and bespectacled face, he continued to preach the gospel of the strenuous life.

What was true of individuals he believed was equally true of nations. The soft, effeminate peoples yielded to the hard masculine ones. The inferior breeds bowed of necessity to the master folk. Roosevelt had studied history seriously. He pictured the past as a contest of elemental forces, with races struggling against one another for dominance. It was necessary to hold that in mind in considering the problems of the present.

The values Roosevelt cherished had been brought into being and developed by the Anglo-Saxons. It was the manliness and virility of the race that had brought the English to their present apogee of glory, and the British Empire was a standing monument to these inherent qualities. But Britain had passed its prime, and the mantle of its leadership was falling to the vigorous new nation of the Western world. The United States was now the repository and guardian of Anglo-Saxon power and culture. More aware than most Americans of the immense resources of his country, Roosevelt was certain that duty and self-interest alike demanded that it take up its obligations as an aggressive force in the world.

England could now no longer bear alone the burden of its heavy responsibilities. In the last decades of the nineteenth century, the great undeveloped areas of the globe had been thrown open to the competition of the rival great powers. The outcome of the struggle was uncertain. Yet it was of the utmost importance that the superior races control the vast resources of Asia and Africa; for those resources would provide the weapons that would command the future mastery of the world. Every now and then Roosevelt teased himself with the horrifying thought that the inferior yellow men or the low Slavic hordes of Russia might turn these massive potentialities to their own use. But generally he had faith that such a disaster could be averted — if only the politicians did not stop at halfway measures. Certainly these considerations made it essential that the United States assume its responsibilities in a positive and unequivocal manner.

Roosevelt also knew by now what the forms of American action must be. He had learned that the key to power in history, from ancient Athens to modern Britain, had been command of the sea. It was by sea, in the past, that force was disposed, conveyed, concentrated, and brought to bear where needed. The navy that controlled the ocean routes determined where power could most effectively be applied. It was therefore of the first importance that the United States acquire a fleet commensurate with its world position.

Sea power, however, entailed more than the accumulation of effective ships. To hold its own a fleet must be able to operate effectively throughout the world. It needed coaling stations and bases that would enable it to defend the nation's commerce, to destroy that of the enemy, and to strike wherever strategic interests dictated. In all these respects the United States was far behind its rivals. Because he was conscious of these necessities, Roosevelt had eagerly accepted the post of Assistant Secretary of the Navy in McKinley's cabinet. Here he imagined he would be in a position to influence the outcome of decisive world events.

Heretofore he had been entirely frustrated. So many opportunities had arisen, only to be passed by!

Through the decade of the 1890's, for instance, Hawaii had literally been begging for annexation. American interests had long been strong in the Islands; missionaries and businessmen had established intimate religious and commercial ties to the United States. The desire to make the archipelago American had provoked a revolution, the dethronement of the Queen, and the creation of a Republic. The strategic value of Hawaii — halfway to Asia — was immense and obvious. But President Cleveland had refused to negotiate for annexation.

His Republican successor was somewhat more receptive to the project. Yet through the spring of 1898 the Hawaiian proposal languished. Commissioners from the Islands had come to the States, prepared to negotiate the terms of annexation. But there was no chance whatsoever that a treaty could command the required two-thirds vote in the Senate; and it was doubtful that even the bare majority needed for a joint resolution could be mustered in both houses.

Yet Hawaii was the key to the central and western Pacific. Roosevelt saw only stupidity and blindness in the failure to seize it. Like other Americans, he thought of the coming struggle for world domination in Asia. The great masses of the Yellow Race, incapable of exploiting their resources or controlling their destiny, were not to be the tools of the grasping states of Europe. They were rather to be guided by the United States. The Americans in such a relationship would gain by adding to their markets the potential purchasing power of 400,000,000 new customers, and find also the opportunity for converting many souls otherwise lost to Christianity. By failing to annex Hawaii, the United States had closed off the high road toward the Orient.

Beyond Hawaii lay a chain of empty, unused islands.

And not far from the coast of Asia were the Philippines, a great archipelago with a population of twenty million, which were going to seed in the hands of the decadent Spaniards. These were the links destined to bind the East to its future American masters. But absolutely nothing was being done at this time to lay hold of them, either as colonies or naval bases.

The same lethargy governed the relationships of the United States with areas closer to hand. If the country were to play its appropriate international role, it was vitally necessary that its fleet be free to pass from one ocean to the other, by means of a canal across Central America. A French company was now laboriously planning to cut a way through at Panama, but the national interest demanded that this channel be someday controlled by the United States. Furthermore, it was important already to give thought to the means of protecting the canal, once it had been built and had become American. Too many foreign powers had footholds in the Caribbean. Yet here, too, the United States had been dilatory.

Cuba provided the golden opportunity for action. For more than a half-century, American statesmen had cast covetous glances at the rich island. Misgoverned by Spain, its valuable resources were being wasted; and there was always the danger that the weak Spanish Government, incapable of retaining control, might transfer its possession to some stronger power hostile to the United States. For this reason alone, altogether apart from its growing investments there, the United States was vitally concerned with the future of Cuba.

For three years the island had been torn by a bitter rebellion. Falling sugar prices had spread economic misery through the land, and the monumental incompetence of the officials had driven the population to desperate extremes. Savage actions by the revolutionaries led to equally savage retaliations. Meanwhile, a junta in New York labored to enlist American sympathies on behalf of the Cubans. This shadow government enlisted men, attempted to ship arms to the revolutionaries, and, most important of all, embarked upon an extensive propaganda campaign to convince Americans of the necessity for intervention.

Cuba thus became a godsend to popular newspapers. William Randolph Hearst's *Journal* and Joseph Pulitzer's *World*, battling for dominance in New York circulation, fastened upon the issue. Exciting stories set forth in horrifying detail the record of Spanish atrocities and whipped popular sentiment to a boiling point.

Americans were prepared to believe the worst of Spain. Their own history of wars along the frontier, stories of the Inquisition, and their latent anti-Catholicism, joined in forming the stereotype of the savage Spaniard. The readers of the *World* and *Journal* could well believe the stories of the brutal concentration camps. Pity for the pathetic victims of "Butcher" Weyler, the Governor-General of the island, combined with a long-standing sympathy with the cause of peoples struggling for independence to produce a sense of American responsibility for the tragedy in Cuba.

Near the end of 1897, Roosevelt had earnestly hoped that the United States might intervene by declaring war; the country needed a good fight. But McKinley had hesitated and let the opportunity pass.

In the following February, after the explosion of the *Maine*, no further delay seemed even thinkable. And yet delay there was. The Assistant Secretary's despondence, in the early days of April, 1898, was certainly understandable.

As Roosevelt considered his colleagues in the government, his contempt at their ineffectuality mounted. His immediate superior was John Davis Long, an amiable gentleman whose memory kept running back to a Maine childhood, to worthy public service as Governor of Massachusetts and as Congressman from that state, to a successful career in the practice of law. Long regarded his cabinet post as a reward and not as a challenge. This man of unimpeachable integrity had no desire for innovation; his ideal was quiet enjoyment of the dignity of his office. A few years earlier he had suffered from a nervous breakdown and now was gingerly caring for himself. Fond of frequent vacations, he was scarcely the leader to create the aggressive fighting force of which his assistant dreamed.

Now and then, therefore, Roosevelt was tempted to appeal over the head of the Secretary of the Navy to the President himself, and occasionally had done so. But the President was, if anything, more cautious! William McKinley had served in the House, but he had given hardly a thought to foreign affairs. His whole concern in office until 1897 had been with domestic problems, notably with those of the tariff and the currency, in regard to which he had always held eminently sound and conservative views. Somewhat to his own surprise he had been singled out for the presidential nomination in 1896; and had fought the campaign against Bryan on the silver question.

What transpired beyond the borders of the continental United States was distinctly foreign to McKinley; diplomacy he thought a matter of no importance. When he took office he had assured Carl Schurz there would be "no jingo nonsense" under his administration, and had vigorously proclaimed his opposition to the acquisition of any new territory "not on the main land," not "Cuba, Hawaii, San Domingo, or any other." McKinley, like Long, was by Roosevelt's standards a weak man, with the backbone of a chocolate éclair. Indecisive, cautious, and timorous in his judgments, the President was likely to rely upon prayer rather than on the force of his own will.

But even the strong men were not reliable! Those in power seemed to Roosevelt blinded by erroneous standards. Behind McKinley loomed the shadowy fig-

ure of his long-time friend and sponsor, Marcus A.
Hanna. Hanna was neither a weakling nor a fool; nor
was he inattentive to his own interests. He dominated
the city of Cleveland and the state of Ohio. After
making a fortune in steel and shipping, he had moved
into politics and had chosen a seat in the Senate as the
vantage point from which to influence the affairs of
the nation. A big man in every sense, he was accustomed to command respect, and he had displayed little
patience with the eccentricities of the younger Roosevelt.

Hanna's power had grown steadily over the years.
It was he who had picked out McKinley and had had
him elected, and the latter remained grateful for and
dependent on the advice of the stronger man. Yet
Hanna, to Roosevelt's intense vexation, could not see
beyond the borders of the United States. Visions of
empire beyond the oceans attracted him not in the
least. Armament and war, he thought, were destructive,
bad for business, and therefore to be avoided. Consistently Hanna was for peace.

Roosevelt came to identify Hanna, as he came to
know him, with the men of new wealth. New Yorker
that he was and sharing the faintly aristocratic pretensions of his family, he tended to look down his nose
at accumulators of mere wealth. Later, his friend
Brooks Adams would explain that the millionaires were
moved by commercial instincts and were the natural
opponents of the warriors with whom Roosevelt aligned

himself. Yet it was these glorified shopkeepers who controlled the government and who stood behind the weaker politicians who did their bidding.

Dissatisfied though he was, the Assistant Secretary did not now conceive the possibility of deserting the Republican Party. He had learned the necessity of regularity as far back as 1884, when he had swallowed his principles and supported Blaine. In the Democratic camp, furthermore, the influence of Bryan was dominant, more pernicious than anything Republican. The young Nebraskan was all that Roosevelt detested. He was a Westerner — not the natural cowboy whom Roosevelt admired, but a city lawyer who lived off the men who fought the wilderness. Bryan was vague in his ideas, pompous in his oratory, and he never convinced Roosevelt of his underlying sincerity. The Democratic standard-bearer had not defined a position on foreign policy. But instinctively Roosevelt distrusted him, suspecting that Bryan was the kind of man who would vote for peace every time.

Only a handful of intimates grasped Roosevelt's vision of the character of coming events; and only to them could he unburden himself in conversation or in correspondence. One of these was his old Harvard friend, Henry Cabot Lodge, now the Junior Senator from Massachusetts. With him Roosevelt could be frank in expressing his fears and frustrations and be assured of an attentive hearing from a kindred spirit. Lodge prided himself upon being the scholar in politics. A student of Henry Adams, and an historian, he had abandoned a successful career at Harvard to become Daniel Webster's disciple in politics. A vain man by nature, he underestimated his genuine learning in some fields, and overestimated his intellectual and political powers in others.

Circumstances now compelled him to fill an uncongenial role. Neither the Senate nor the Commonwealth of Massachusetts was what it had been in Webster's day; Lodge's position in both prevented him from playing the part of the orator, and forced him instead to play the backstairs manipulator. He was nowhere at home, except perhaps in the rocky withdrawal of Nahant. In his own state he felt increasingly uncomfortable among the motley group of politicians — including the Irish — on whose support he depended. In the Senate he was equally unfamiliar and ill at ease with the bustling politicians of the rude West who formed its majority. He, who felt himself to be all that was truly American, always wore the badge of his strangeness and alienation. For him Roosevelt was the one oasis of friendship in the wilderness of Washington.

In the easy exchange of ideas, the two discovered the extent of their agreement — on the importance of racial forces in history, on their joint dislike of and yet desire to emulate England, and on their common conception of the imperial destiny of the United States.

Older than either of these two politicians was the

naval officer with whom they occasionally exchanged confidences. Captain Alfred Thayer Mahan was an anomaly. In a service that prided itself on roughness and bluntness, he was a scholar who not only read but also wrote books. He had attained no distinction in action; and in the uneventful years of his service had not had the opportunity to rise. The Navy had not grown since the Civil War and Mahan was only a captain at the time of his retirement. Actually he disliked shipboard life and his dreams of glory led him from off the deck to bury himself in study of naval history. Among his books, he spun out those theories of naval power that Theodore Roosevelt found so attractive.

With these men Theodore Roosevelt discussed the problems of the long anticipated war, although its prospects seemed remote even with the sinking of the *Maine* in early 1898. Already the strategic moment had passed. The war should have come in November or December. Then the United States might have overthrown the tottering Spanish empire without the least difficulty. With every month that went by, Roosevelt feared, Spain grew stronger while the United States stood still. Hence the desperation with which he watched time fly.

There was another cause for concern. Even if the plight of Cuba should at last induce the Americans to intervene, there was no assurance that any permanent result would follow. Swayed by soft humanitarian impulses, the country's leaders were likely to regard the war as no more than a step toward Cuban independence. They might well fail to understand that it ought also to be the means of establishing an American empire.

Again and again, the Assistant Secretary's thoughts turned to the Far East. The newspaper headlines shrieked of Cuba, but he was convinced that the nation's future lay in the Orient. The country must therefore be prepared to capitalize upon any favorable situation. If war should come, the United States must wrest from Spain an imperial position in the Pacific. More important than Cuba as an objective were the Philippines. For a year, Roosevelt had secretly been laying plans for their conquest.

For a long time past the United States Navy had operated a China squadron in Far Eastern waters. Its function had been simple enough, to maintain American prestige and to protect occasional merchantmen. The Assistant Secretary was determined to turn it into an effective striking force, his weapon of assault against the Philippines.

To this end, he began looking for an appropriate commander in 1897, and through a comic misapprehension he soon found him in Commodore George Dewey. Dewey was a Vermonter, then approaching his sixtieth birthday. He had not seen sea duty for almost ten years. A liver ailment had brought him ashore, and he had contrived a pleasant life for himself in the routine of successive Washington offices. A widower, and a man of regular habits, his tastes ran to elegant clothes and good horses. It was this gentleman, who enjoyed lingering over dinner at the Metropolitan Club, who was Roosevelt's unlikely candidate for the hero's role in the Pacific.

Dewey had come to the Assistant Secretary's attention through a story which was a good one, even if apocryphal. Somewhere, Roosevelt had picked up the report that Dewey had almost single-handedly launched a war against Chile. Such daring, beyond the call of duty or the strict letter of his orders, was a sure sign of the personal qualities that Roosevelt sought in an officer. The impression of recklessness was confirmed by another rumor — equally unfounded — according to which Dewey had single-handedly quelled a mutiny on the *Dolphin*.

This was enough for the Assistant Secretary. Through his influence Dewey was translated from a desk in the Board of Surveys to the deck of the flagship *Olympia*. In January, 1898, the new commander reached his fleet in Nagasaki and forthwith led it off to Hong Kong.

That was an additional reason for Roosevelt's impatience in the spring of 1898. Now the man and the ships were where they should be. Let them only be prepared to fight!

On several occasions, Roosevelt had mentioned to Secretary Long the desirability of having Dewey in readiness to move toward the Philippines should hostilities begin. Long regarded the suggestion as preposterous. The war might be avoided altogether; and if it were not, it would be confined to Cuba. The place for the fleet then would be the Caribbean and not the Western Pacific.

Fatigued by the running conflict with the belligerent Roosevelt, the easygoing Secretary decided to take the day off at home on February 25. Perhaps he was a little uneasy as to what might happen in his absence. In any case, he took the precaution of warning his impetuous subordinate to take no rash action alone. Long, alas, was mistaken in believing that such a warning at such a time would be in the least effective.

In temporary command of the department, Roosevelt resolved, come what might, to make the most of his brief tenure of power. On February 25 he dispatched a confidential cable to Dewey at Hong Kong. The Commodore was to remain in constant readiness, adequately coaled up and supplied, and was to strike at the Spaniards in the Philippines the moment news of a declaration of war arrived. There is no indication this message would have been approved by the Secretary or the President. Yet it was to transform a struggle for Cuban independence into a war for American empire. Ultimately, it would shatter the continental limits of American responsibilities and push the United States into a position in the world for which it was scarcely prepared.

All this while, the President had been wrestling with the problems of intervention. The growing clamor for assistance to the Cuban rebels drove him toward action; but his own conservatism resisted. The great mass dailies, led by the *Journal* and *World,* were in a frenzy of excitement. Yet McKinley realized that a peaceful solution was in sight.

The liberal Sagasta ministry was now in power in Spain. Fully aware of its country's weakness, it was pathetically eager to appease the Yankees. But as was so often the case on the Continent in those decades, the liberals were free only to take the blame for the disasters they had inherited. Sagasta hastened to make any concession that would allow him to keep peace in the Caribbean and still save face at home — autonomy, independence, an armistice, anything.

An acquiescent spirit spread through Madrid. The Spaniards realized that they could not alone oppose the Americans, and they had been unable to find support for force in Europe. The great powers were sympathetic toward Spain, and at one point appealed to McKinley for peace. But no one wished to antagonize the United States by giving aid to the languishing Spanish empire.

In Germany the young Kaiser, Wilhelm II, had recently begun to direct the affairs of his government. He for one sympathized with the Spaniards and disliked the Americans, but he was too much involved to act unilaterally on behalf of Madrid. His cousin Nicky, the

Czar of Russia, was also a newcomer to the throne and lacked confidence. Nor was the shaky French Republic, torn asunder by the Dreyfus affair, or the tottering Austro-Hungarian Empire, already laboring under the stresses of mounting nationalistic dissensions, any more likely to act. All depended on the decision of England.

In London Queen Victoria was sympathetic to the Queen Regent of Spain, a woman about to lose an empire. But larger considerations than the whims of the venerable lady shaped British policy. Lord Salisbury, a hardheaded peer schooled under Disraeli, would not tolerate the least sign of sentimentality in diplomacy. Almost seventy, he had already had thirty years of experience as a negotiator. As German and Russian power mounted, he decided that the future security of the British Empire reposed on friendship with the United States. In the Venezuela crisis three years earlier, he had made his choice, and now encouraged rather than restrained the Americans. There was thus no hope for the Spaniards.

Sagasta's readiness to grant concessions, however, made the war difficult to come at. Yet war there was to be. For a martial madness had swept over a large part of the United States and to it the President had finally succumbed. Torn by indecision, he had at last sunk to his knees in prayer and risen with the conviction that the war must come. Thus the people would be satisfied and a righteous cause served. On April 11, McKinley asked for and a week later received from

Congress a declaration of war on behalf of the independence of Cuba.

While general attention was now concentrated on the Caribbean, the more significant happenings were in the Pacific as a result of Roosevelt's forethought, especially his dispatch of February 25. Dewey, an officer of habit and order, had obeyed and was ready. News of the declaration of war duly reached Hong Kong on April 24. That was Dewey's signal. He waited only to pick up the American consul, who had already left the Philippines and who might have useful information. Then, on April 27, the Asiatic squadron set forth for Luzon, six hundred miles away.

In the evening of April 30, the American ships approached the harbor of Manila Bay, where the long history of the Spanish Empire was about to come to an end. These waters had once seen Magellan's battered vessel riding at anchor; through them had passed the galleons on the way to Spain with the fabled wealth of the East. Now they would see the birth of a new imperial power.

It was almost ten o'clock of a dark night when Dewey came up to the approaches to the harbor. He floated silently by, within reach of the guns on the great island fortress Corregidor. He met no resistance. The defenders of the Philippines were simply not prepared. Even when the soot in the smokestack of the *McCulloch* burst into flame and illuminated the advancing fleet, only a few desultory shots, altogether ineffective, greeted it. At daybreak, the Americans were in the bay, prepared for the first and final battle.

At four o'clock in the morning the Americans had hot coffee and hardtack, and approached the Spanish fleet anchored off the naval base at Cavite. Dewey, wearing a golfer's cap — for he had mislaid his splendid uniform cap — led the flotilla to within five thousand yards of the enemy. Then, at 5:40 A.M., he turned parallel to the anchored Spaniards, and gave the order to fire.

The enemy was still not ready. The American ships, in line, passed from west to east, hailing shells down upon the motionless Spanish vessels. Circling, Dewey returned, his guns ablaze and now encountering occasional return fire from the enemy. Five times, in the next two and a half hours, Dewey passed back and forth with little danger and no damage to himself. Dense columns of smoke rose above the harbor and obscured the scene. A pall of dark smoke thrown up by the exploding gunpowder hung between the attackers and Cavite. Dewey had no idea whatsoever whether his firing was accurate or whether it matched that of the Spaniards in ineffectiveness.

Then Dewey received the disquieting word that he had only fifteen rounds of ammunition left. Suddenly his position had become precarious. Far from any base, he was exposed to disastrous retaliation. Quickly he gave the order to draw off and to prepare for a consultation. The Americans moved back down the bay.

There had been an error. Someone had miscounted. Fully forty-five rounds remained, so that battle could be resumed. Only the Commodore was eager to find a creditable reason for the temporary withdrawal, one that would satisfy public opinion. Joseph L. Stickney, a newspaperman, conveniently present, supplied it. Dewey announced that he had moved back to partake of a quiet breakfast; and as the men rested, the basis of a legend of imperturbability was laid that would make Dewey famous.

At eleven o'clock the American fleet returned to action. By then the pall of smoke had lifted, exposing the wrecks of the Spanish vessels. A few additional rounds brought capitulation at noon. By August 13 Manila too had fallen, and the Philippines passed to the control of the Americans.

It had been a splendid battle. No American casualties, no American losses, a decisive Spanish defeat! The news when it reached home earned Dewey overwhelming popularity. It also brought to the attention of the delirious people the existence of a part of the world of which few had theretofore heard. Acquired so gallantly, without cost of lives, the Philippines were to become American, whatever price in gold was to be paid after the peace. The settlement would also give the conquerors Puerto Rico and a larger stake in the Caribbean than those eager to liberate Cuba had envisioned.

The United States was thus to be committed, for the next few years to a policy of imperialism, and forever to a global destiny. If that destiny was somewhat different from what Theodore Roosevelt had dreamed of during the winter and the spring of 1898, it was nevertheless, in large measure, a product of his daring dispatch to Hong Kong.

CHAPTER SEVEN

The *Lusitania*

THOSE who watched from the pier knew the emotions usual at sailings. They felt the initial pain of separation as the gangplanks dropped away and the first feet of clearing water divided them from those who were departing. Then, as the eye's focus shifted from the waving figures at the railing and took in the majestic whole of the ship now pulling back into the river, with its graceful lines beneath the gay banners fluttering from its masts, those who had been left behind felt the sting of envy as they imagined the adventure, the gaiety, and the fun that awaited those aboard during the week of freedom ahead of them.

Envy and regret were the dominant emotions on May 1, 1915, as the Cunarder *Lusitania* set sail from New York. A new summer season was about to begin, and many of those who stood on the dock were themselves anticipating the coming joy of a tour, despite the ugly war in Europe. To the shouted farewells were frequently added the promises of meetings somewhere across the ocean.

There were no forebodings. Those who had found

time to glance through the morning's newspapers may have noticed an official German advertisement: Americans were warned that a war zone existed around the British Isles and that they sailed on Allied vessels at their own risk. But that grim announcement attracted little attention then.

Neither those who sailed nor those who stayed behind suffered the anxieties of the threat of danger. In a few months' time the great war in Europe would be a year old; and Americans had already become accustomed to its costs in blood and money, to its fluctuating victories and defeats. That it might touch civilians embarked on a noncombatant ship was unimaginable — ungallant as well as illegal, in an age that still associated gallantry and legality with war.

The *Lusitania* never reached port. The shock of its sinking — the first outraged perception of what modern war meant — turned Americans onto a course that led them further through war to an unwilling new role in a wider world.

The great vessel had been then less than eight years in service. The pride of the British merchant fleet, it was a world removed from the grimy uncomfortable craft that only a generation earlier had ferried passengers across the Atlantic. Sea travel by now had been embellished with elegance and grace; the trim decks were made for the leisurely stroll of unworried vacationers, and the concern for comfort hid every evidence that it was still the business of ships to carry goods.

In the last decades of the nineteenth century the great powers, engaged in an obsessive naval race, discovered that it was in the national interest to build up the size of their merchant marine. Competition from the French and Germans and Italians compelled Great Britain to fight bitterly to retain its supremacy. Direct government subsidies were everywhere thrown into the battle and relieved shipbuilders and shipowners of the necessity of taking account of costs in the effort to attract passengers.

There followed golden years. The floating palaces grew steadily in size and added luxury after luxury to their accouterments. Borrowing the style of the flamboyant resorts of the period, the designers outdid themselves in the provisions for stylish public rooms and comfortable cabins. The cuisine was an orgy of Edwardian self-indulgence, with provision for the anticipation of every possible desire.

Yet, magically, the subsidies kept the cost of travel relatively low. An ocean voyage, once undertaken only out of necessity or daring, now became part of the commonplace glamour of a European tour. The gaily jostling dancers who so often waltzed the whole journey across never troubled to think that the subsidies had a purpose, and that that purpose was war.

The *Lusitania* had been commissioned at the height of the naval race; the plans approved by the Admiralty, and the cost underwritten by the British treasury. The ship was intended once and for all to demonstrate the maritime superiority of the Union Jack. This was to be the largest, swiftest, most comfortable passenger vessel in commission. She had come down the ways at Clydebank in June, 1906, built by John Brown and Company. More than a year had then been spent in fitting her out. When she sailed in September, 1907, on her maiden voyage, she was endowed with every attribute for speed and safety that British engineering could devise. She carried off the blue ribbon with ease.

Most often she appeared in photographs and drawings coming out of the picture toward the viewer. Her bow rose high in the foreground while the deckline seemed to slope down toward the distant horizon in an approximate indication of her immense size. The four smokestacks that somewhat unaesthetically broke the harmony of her silhouette nevertheless left an impression of immense power. She was 785 feet long and 85 feet wide and was registered at 40,000 tons. She could carry 2000 passengers and a crew of 600, and did 25 knots without difficulty.

The *Lusitania* had been popular from the start. If she carried less than capacity on this trip, it was not so much because of the war, as because the season had hardly started and because on eastbound voyages the steerage space reserved for the immigrant trade was usually unoccupied. As it was, the ship's passenger list ran to 1250 names, 188 of them American citizens.

The trip was uneventful. Shipboard life ran its usual carefree course. The travelers enjoyed the relaxing sense of detachment, within their own closed world, from the old problems they had left behind and the new ones they were approaching. The war news hardly intruded, and the crew was studiously determined to carry on imperturbably as if nothing mattered but the self-contained life of the ship.

That determination stemmed from a decision of the ship's commander, Captain W. H. Turner. At best, the role of such a man was difficult and ambiguous. His responsibilities were numerous and not always compatible with one another. He was charged with the supervision of the complex operations of the vessel and of its large crew. It was his duty to bring his craft safely to harbor. On the other hand, he was also obliged to make the voyage as pleasant as possible for the passengers. In his planning he had always to take account of the comfort and convenience of the thousand strangers on board who were, in a manner of speaking, his guests. Often, when adjusting his uniform in the morning, such a man could hardly be certain whether it was an Elizabethan seadog or a headwaiter at the Ritz who faced him in the mirror.

The war made the dilemma more difficult. Captain Turner himself bore a commission in the naval reserves and might be called to active service at any time. He had no illusions about the seriousness of the fighting. A sister ship, the *Mauretania,* had already been converted to a troop carrier; the *Lusitania* might soon have to answer a similar summons. Indeed, as he watched more than four thousand cases of ammunition come aboard in New York, he might have reflected that the ship was already doing its part. More than half his cargo was involved in the war effort.

Captain Turner knew also that the war was not a remote land-bound affair, but one capable of washing up against the sides of his own vessel. He had read the decrees of the Imperial German Government, proclaiming a zone around the British Isles within which the merchantmen of belligerents would be attacked; and before him were instructions from the Admiralty as to how to minimize risks. He was directed to shun the usual route, to take a zigzag course, to be constantly alert, and to ram enemy submarines if he saw them.

The captain felt uneasy in the face of these directions. Orders were orders. But then, he had other obligations as well. He could envisage the subtle spread of panic among the passengers if the change of course became known, the piercing fears that would pervade the lounges if the ship started zigzagging. Delay might upset the ship's schedule, and in any case the stimulated tension would spoil the journey. Was it really necessary?

Perhaps, in forming an answer, he thought back to another incident three months earlier, when a sudden alarm had induced him to lower his own flag and to come into Liverpool flying the American colors. He had not liked that. Perhaps, as he stepped out of the cabin and surveyed the magnificent strength of the *Lusitania*, his pride would not allow him to believe that she could really be destroyed. Perhaps it was only a quick resolution to take a chance. One way or another, the decision was made: the vessel followed its usual route and ignored the Admiralty instructions.

On the morning of May 7, the Irish coast loomed on the horizon. The trip had been uneventful and the risk, it seemed, had been worth taking.

Another captain approached a rendezvous at the same spot that day. Lieutenant Commander Schweiger of the Imperial German Navy had left his base in Emden in the middle of March. His instructions were to lurk unobserved in the Irish Sea and its channels, and to attack British shipping plying in and out of Liverpool. So far he had not had much luck in his two-month cruise.

Indeed, as he somewhat glumly contemplated his situation in early May, Schweiger concluded that he had very little luck in his military career. German naval men often thought of themselves with self-pity. In their own country they were distinctly the junior service; all the honor and the glory and the rewards went to the army. When they compared themselves with their British counterparts, there was always a trace of envy at the consciousness of the vast social esteem and power that the latter enjoyed, but which they did not.

Of all naval officers, Schweiger thought himself the least fortunate. He had not even a respectable vessel to command, not even a decent wardroom in which to serve. His ship, alas, was neither elegant nor commodious. The *U-20* was a submarine, an untested newcomer among naval craft and no object of respect to those who, like himself, dreamed of berths on the battleships and cruisers that were the pride of the fleet.

As the weeks dragged by, Schweiger's patience had worn thin, and his physical energy was running out.

He had attacked a few small British vessels and sunk some of them, but they were nothing worth boasting about. Other than that there had been a great deal of hard labor in the narrow confines of the tiny boat. The men were tired, supplies were running low, and further continuation of the cruise seemed pointless.

Most of all the submarine's crew worried about its vulnerability. Apart from the concern over a new device, the principle of which they barely understood, they could see for themselves that it was not much of a ship for a fight. Even if they could always rely on its coming up after it had gone down, it was no match for any warship or even for any armed merchantman. It was painfully slow; fortunate, indeed, if it could get up to twelve knots. Its armor was paper thin. Attacked, it could not even withdraw to the safety of submersion, for it could operate only close to the surface of the water. A single hit from even a small gun was likely to be fatal; and a vessel of moderate size used as a ram could crush the submarine like an eggshell.

Such thoughts rushed through Schweiger's mind when he seized a 99-ton schooner toward the end of April. As he stood by to let the crew take to lifeboats before sinking his prize, he nervously reflected on his own vulnerable and exposed position.

The state of jitters persisted. Early in May, as his fuel sank to the danger point, Schweiger determined to head for home. The trip was hazardous. The waters of the channel and the North Sea were strewn with mines, and English naval craft were everywhere. Constant vigilance was essential. Schweiger kept his eye glued to the periscope.

On May 7 the silhouette of a large ship loomed up suddenly before him in the lens.

The first part of May, 1915, was a time of concern in Europe, not so much for the public which everywhere still had the heart to accept the optimistic headlines of the press, but for the handful of men in each of the warring nations who understood that crucial decisions were in the making. On both sides the first crafty calculations of quick victory had been exploded. The overconfident blueprints of conquest had been laid aside as control passed into the hands of sober soldiers and politicians who understood that the war would be long and hard.

A somber mood hung over London. Nine months before Foreign Secretary Grey had seen the lights go out all over Europe and had marked it down as the beginning of the end of the world that he had known. There was no cause for greater optimism now. The first German thrusts had been repulsed. But the ultimate outcome was still unclear.

On land Allied strategic leadership was in the hands of the French. But naval policy was the British province, and the Admiralty had adopted the classical tactics of combat with a continental power. If the Germans could but be held back, sea power in time would be decisive. A tight blockade would cut the Kaiser off from essential supplies, weaken his economy, sap the strength of his army, and leave him exposed to a crushing knockout blow. So Napoleon's empire had been crushed a century earlier.

The parallel was not altogether reassuring. Napoleon had been beaten without a drain on Britain's own manpower. This time the flower of Britain's youth was being sacrificed on European battlefields. Few statesmen now were confident that England could afford a quarter-century of conflict. Unrest in Ireland and India betrayed a growing weakness in the Empire and the rising strength of the Labor Party was a sign of instability at home. Meanwhile, the French and Russian partners were regarded without enthusiasm — useful but not altogether dependable. Many an Englishman now thought the country's best hope for the future lay in strengthening its understanding with the United States.

The longstanding enmity between the former colony and the mother country had begun to abate toward the end of the nineteenth century. Old grievances had been settled and English statesmen had gone out of their way to pay court to Americans. Now and then the hope was even expressed that some day the transatlantic breach would be healed and some form of Union would draw together the two "Anglo-Saxon" powers.

The outbreak of war made the rapprochement crucial, for the United States was the most powerful neutral on earth. The British launched an intensive propaganda campaign to win over the Americans to an understanding of the Teutonic menace to civilization. American aid in the form of munitions and money began to flow across the Atlantic.

But that was not enough for the British. The United States remained stubbornly neutral. What was more, its legalistic protests against the blockade of Germany threatened to spike that essential weapon against the Central Powers.

No one felt this more strongly than the King. George V was a relative newcomer to the throne. He lacked the distinctive qualities of his two immediate predecessors and was therefore sometimes taken for a cipher, which he was not. Quiet in manner and reticent in speech, he nevertheless saw issues in clear-cut categories and was capable of acting with decision when the occasion called for it.

George was thoroughly wrapped up in the war. He saw an appropriateness to his role as wartime leader of his people and was convinced of the righteousness of his cause. He had never liked his distant cousin the Kaiser and was prepared to believe the worst about German intentions. By 1915 he was convinced that England was battling on behalf of all the decencies and was impatient with those who did not understand the necessity of aiding her. The American attitude of neutrality he considered thoroughly obtuse, for it did not recognize the absolute malevolence of the Germans. If only, he often thought, some dramatic event would make clear the danger to civilization! "Suppose," he said to Colonel House one day in May, 1915, "suppose they should sink the *Lusitania* with American passengers on board?"

For the Germans the war had begun with a series of ponderous miscalculations. All their lives the members of the General Staff and the Kaiser's elaborate corps of imperial advisers had labored to reduce the manifold possibilities of international politics to a scientific system, mathematically coherent enough to take account of every contingency. Assuming that power A acted, while B and C did not, and E remained indecisive, then we in conjunction with F must move into phase G, prepared to deploy, on day H at I hour,

J men according to scheme K. So ran the elaborate plans they spun, abstract from any immediate human consideration.

Hemmed in by formulae, and bound by the cast-iron obligations of alliances, they seemed to have lost their freedom of diplomatic maneuver. In the complex pattern of the European balance of power every event had its necessary response. If the Russians mobilized, the Germans had to declare war. If the French came in in support of the Russians, the quick thrust through Belgium was inescapable. It had all been set down in logic so tight there was no crevice through which to wiggle to an alternative.

The Kaiser was as bound as the rest. Truly the head of the state since he had dismissed Bismarck some twenty years earlier, Wilhelm II was consulted on all meaningful decisions. He was still proud as he reflected how speedily Germany had developed in his lifetime, in size, power, wealth and culture. Yet even he could not afford to be capricious and arbitrary; even he accepted the obligations of German diplomacy and military planning.

By the spring of 1915, however, it was sadly apparent that the elaborate plans had miscarried. The Prussian tradition had always looked toward short brisk wars; and in contemplating this one the General Staff had envisaged quick knock-out blows to east and west that would create the conditions for a settlement. No one had foreseen the bloody stalemate that was to bog down great armies as they took to the trenches.

The naval command might have taken quiet satisfaction in the discomfiture of the army, but for the fact that its own expectations were not being realized. The Kaiser had been induced to embark upon an expensive building program, and one that cost him British friendship, by a theory propounded by the head of the German Navy. It was not necessary to outbuild the English, Admiral von Tirpitz had explained. As an island empire dependent on sea power, Great Britain would always insist upon a fleet second to none; and she had the resources to make that insistence real. But Germany did not need as large a navy. Let her but have a force strong enough to do irreparable damage, even if defeated, and that would be deterrent enough.

The theory had been only partially successful. The splendid British battle fleet had indeed cautiously refrained from venturing forth from its base at Scapa Flow. But the blockade imposed by flotillas of destroyers and other small craft might in time choke Germany to death. Meanwhile the Kaiser's navy was hung by its own theory. Designed for a specific purpose, it was not willing to risk damaging encounters with anything less than the British battle fleet and stayed securely within its own safe harbors. Here again there was a stalemate!

For the time being the German naval command limited its operations to the destruction of Allied commerce, hoping thus to counteract the influence of the blockade. It used toward that end whatever miscellaneous corsairs it could scrape together, including a few submarines, then regarded as little more than experimental toys. In February, 1915, a war zone had been proclaimed around the British Isles within which all Allied ships were to be sunk at sight.

In the next few months an occasional sinking brought protests; Germany had after all signed various international conventions, agreeing that passengers be warned and given the opportunity to leave the ships about to be sunk. The advertisement in the New York papers of May 1 had been the response. Travelers intending to embark on the *Lusitania* had had their warning, and their opportunity.

In Washington quite a different view prevailed.

The Democrats had come back to office after sixteen years out of power. None of the party chiefs had much experience with foreign affairs.

The first place in the cabinet had gone to William Jennings Bryan as a reward for his aid in securing Wilson the nomination. Given the circumstances, the appointment was far better than might have been expected.

Having been three times defeated in the quest for the presidency, Bryan was by now no longer the boy orator but an elder statesman. Free silver and many other Populist slogans of the flamboyant past were dead, and Bryan himself had come to understand that the great issues of government were more than just occasions for making speeches. Soberly he set about learning his job, determined to make a durable reputation as Secretary of State.

The central problem was peace. Bryan took office in a period of high hopes. A little earlier Andrew Carnegie, setting up the endowment for international peace, had worried over the disposition of his fund when wars had ceased to exist; so near to the desired goal did men then think they were! The new Secretary launched upon a program designed to further international understanding by arbitration treaties and other measures. When the war came he was terribly disappointed; but he was resolved, like his chief, that American neutrality was the best means of quieting Europe in its feverish state. In this stand he had the support of an influential body of American opinion that included pacifists as well as pro-German and anti-English groups.

On the other hand, by 1915 he had to struggle against powerful elements that were convinced that only an Allied victory was in the American interest. His undersecretary, Robert Lansing, and his ambassador in London, W. H. Page, had become privately committed to the English cause. They supported private war loans to Britain and favored extension of the munitions trade. Most of all they argued that the United

States ought unflinchingly to maintain its rights as a neutral against Germany.

Ultimately the decision was the President's to make, and increasingly he felt the burden of it. Before 1914 Wilson had paid little attention to these matters. As a historian of American politics he had only rarely dealt with diplomacy, and as a politician he had been entirely absorbed in domestic affairs. He had fallen in with Bryan's policy at the start, for his own inclinations were pacific. When the war came he called upon his fellow countrymen to be neutral in thought as well as in deed, and he determined to hold his country apart from the havoc being spread in Europe. In Mexico, too, against the strenuous clamor of those who urged intervention, he pursued a policy of watchful waiting.

Wilson, however, was moved by considerations that did not affect Bryan. His deepest personal sympathies were English; close cultural and social ties with the "mother country" tugged at his heart. Moreover, he was disturbed in an almost religious sense by the moral issues of the contest. War was not right. But it was doubly unrighteous when it led to the violation of treaties and the disregard of international law.

In February, 1915, the German declaration of the war zone — an illegal act — had offended the President. Bryan, foreseeing the consequences, had urged the government to forbid its citizens to expose themselves to risks that were also risks for the whole nation.

But Wilson would not yield. Americans had a perfect right to travel where they wished and on what ships they chose, including those of belligerents; and the United States would hold the Germans strictly accountable for any harm that might befall them.

By May 7 he had not in the least modified this rigid position.

That day Captain Schweiger watched the ship speed across his periscope. Its name was unclear. But it was certainly British and large. A fair prize.

He may have paused a second to consider a warning. If he did, he quickly discarded the idea. The vessel was fast and could easily outspeed and escape him. Or worse, it might turn its guns upon the submarine or ram it to destruction.

The time was short. The tube was ready. He ordered a torpedo released.

As he watched the course of the speeding missile, Schweiger's heart sank in disappointment. The torpedo was obviously wide of its mark.

He had not time, however, to move back from the eyepiece when he noticed the target unaccountably veer and head directly into the path of the approaching torpedo. The torpedo struck home, and the ship quivered from the impact. Slowly she began to sink.

The *U–20* stood back to watch its victim's boats being lowered and to see the passengers taken off. Schweiger could not make out the confusion aboard, the dismay and incomprehension among those who had thought themselves almost safely ashore. He only knew that the work went slowly. Eighteen minutes later a sharp explosion tore the vessel apart. She went down stern foremost. Just before the waters closed over her proud bow, the U-boat commander could at last make out her name. His prize had been the *Lusitania.*

Schweiger went home to a promotion and a medal; this had been the greatest victory of the German submarine campaign.

But the sinking of the *Lusitania* had another deeper significance. Along with the 600 crewmen almost 1200 passengers had perished. A shock of revulsion passed through neutral America. Civilians, it had believed, ought not to be spattered with the blood of the battlefields. Now all the faith in the gallantry of war began to fade; those battles were not limited to the men in arms, but reached out to embrace everyone. And the Germans had been responsible.

Now the stories of the rape of Belgium became all at once credible. In the year to come the most outrageous inventions of the British propaganda service would be swallowed without question. The stain left on German *Kultur* would not out. Shortly the ambassador in Washington advised his government that German counterpropaganda was altogether futile. No one believed it.

Among those who went down with the *Lusitania* were more than one hundred Americans. Their death was a direct challenge to the President who had said that he would hold the Germans strictly accountable for such loss of lives. For almost two years the government of the United States tried to get Berlin to accept responsibility and to make adequate reparations. The Germans would not yield. The long involved exchange of notes further poisoned relationships between the two states and was only terminated by the outbreak of war.

For the President, however, still more was involved. A principle was at stake. The submarine campaign flouted international law. To him that was clear while all else was dark and confused. The seesaw of armies across Europe made the future of that continent uncertain. Menacing moves by the Japanese threatened the stability of Asia. At home there was a brief recession, and the American economy became ever more meshed in with the needs of the Allied war machines. Meanwhile, a confused clamor from discordant influences attempted to sway his actions. But the principle to which he could adhere was clear. It might impose on him burdensome obligations; but let him act in accord with it, and he would know he was right.

To the hotheads who urged immediate war the President spoke at Philadelphia three days after the sinking of the *Lusitania*. "There is such a thing," he said, "as a man being too proud to fight. There is such a thing as a nation being so right that it does not need to convince others by force that it is right." The statement did not mean that the United States would not fight, but that it would not fight out of pride and that it would maintain the righteousness of its position without force.

But what if the others refused to be convinced, refused even to discuss the issue in terms of right and wrong?

By the end of the month the German Government had rejected the first American note of protest, maintaining that the attack on the *Lusitania* was an act of "just self-defense" and rejecting entirely the President's contention that it was responsible for the loss of lives.

The President himself set the terms of the American rejoinder. It was phrased in words so strong that Bryan refused to sign it. The note took a position from which the United States would not in the future be able to recede, one from which there could be no response to a German rebuff but war. The Secretary of State feared the dangerous slope down which the nation was plunging and resigned rather than send off the message. Lansing, his successor, needed no convincing and was more compliant.

Wilson did not think that war would follow, and he was right. The Germans preferred to spin out the discussions over months, and finally, almost a year after the *Lusitania* went down, announced the suspension of the submarine campaign.

This turn of policy was not due, however, to acceptance of Wilson's principle or to rejection of the submarine as a weapon. The Kaiser at that juncture wished to keep the Americans mollified while the summer campaigns, newly planned, brought him victory. The issue fell into temporary abeyance, and Wilson could in good earnest claim in the campaign of that year that he had kept us out of war. Nonetheless, he now and then expressed his uneasiness; he had not withdrawn from the advanced position of the *Lusitania* notes, and another shift in German policy might compel him to move on to the action he did not wish to contemplate.

In the fall and winter of 1916 the memory of the *Lusitania* was vivid also in other minds. The German columns moving forward were everywhere at length stopped; the snow began to cover Europe with the war still unended. More than ever it was necessary to break out of the vise of the blockade and to cut the revivifying flow of supplies that kept the Allies strong. The naval command thought back to the achievement of the *U–20*. How readily the tiny craft with its handful of men had destroyed the 40,000-ton pride of the British merchant marine! A few score submarines thrown into the battle now might turn the tide.

The Kaiser's government weighed the risk. More certainly than Wilson himself they realized that this would mean war with the United States. But the Americans were remote and not mobilized; they could hardly make ready in time to affect the course of events. And the decisive calculation was this: the *Lusitania* had shown that submarines could be built far more quickly than the ships they destroyed. At the end of January, 1917, the Imperial German Government gave notice that it was about to resume unrestricted submarine warfare.

For Wilson the long struggle for neutrality was ended. A man of peace, he had a hatred for war; and better than most of his contemporaries he could foresee what the costs of war would be. Yet as Bryan had predicted, the stand taken in the heat of indignation at the sinking of the *Lusitania* compelled the President now to treat the resumption of submarine operations as an aggressive act directed against the United States. Wilson could not withdraw without an unbearable sacrifice of principle. Diplomatic relations were cut at once, and shortly a formal declaration of war associated the United States with the Allied Powers.

For Wilson, who moved reluctantly toward it, and for many Americans who welcomed their involvement innocently, almost gaily, the destruction of the *Lusitania* had been a turning point. Had the ship made a safe landing and Captain Schweiger proceeded disconsolately home, millions of Americans might not then have recognized the horrifying face of modern war. And without the mood of revulsion that followed, the government might not then have committed itself to a course that in time led the nation unprepared into the midst of the fighting and the long chain of consequences that followed.

CHAPTER EIGHT

Pearl Harbor

LATER every man would enshrine in his own memory the particular circumstance attending the announcement of the news. To all but a few this Sunday began like any other, given to late sleeping or churchgoing, to idle turning of the newspaper pages, to the easy somnolence of the hour after the family dinner. Then a neighbor came banging at the door, or the telephone rang, or someone thought to turn the radio on. The world was never again the same.

For some Americans the change had already begun.

In the very early morning of December 7 in the waters off Hawaii the crew of the *U.S.S. Ward* sensed it. The destroyer was manned almost entirely by boys out of the reserves, hesitant and somewhat unsure of themselves. But their detecting devices had picked up the shape of a submarine where they knew that none should be. At 6:45 A.M. Lieutenant Commander Outerbridge ordered the strange craft attacked and destroyed. He reported the incident to Pearl Harbor, and sometime later the report was read — too late. He did not know then that another submarine that had no business there had already entered the great naval base.

As noon approached messages came down from the control towers: unidentified aircraft were approaching the Islands. Before the warnings were read the bombers were overhead. No defending planes rose to meet them. The low-flying attackers tore apart the rows of airplanes neatly arrayed on the ramps and shot on to destroy the United States Pacific Fleet riding at anchor in the harbor. As the intruders turned back to their carriers, the striking power of the American Navy was gone. As a result all of southeastern Asia for a time fell to the Japanese, and that left its tragic impress on the war and on the peace that followed.

Often in the months of bitter sacrifice before the war was won the nation's leaders thought back to this turning point, their minds burdened with a question. Why had the attack succeeded? It was not enough to answer because it was a surprise. The enemy's hostile intentions were well enough known. The attack succeeded rather because chance permitted a lucky foe to worm through an old gap between our diplomacy and our naval policy.

Only the night before at dinner President Roosevelt had read the secret document gravely. Tired of the long weeks of uncertainty, he had turned to Harry Hopkins and said, "This means war."

Almost four and a half years had gone by since the issue first had presented itself, and the President had felt the mark of these passing years. He was not so jaunty now or self-confident; the sobering events since 1937 had given him some insight into the intractable forces generated when the interests of nations collided. He was still tempted toward an optimistic faith in the persuasive powers of reasonableness; but those temptations were now checked by the recollection of unhappy experiences.

All these problems had seemed much clearer in October, 1937, when he had called in Chicago for a quarantine of aggressors. In July of that year, the incident at the Marco Polo Bridge in Peking had given the Japanese the excuse to invade China proper. The President had spoken his mind in decisive and unambiguous terms.

Nothing thereafter had the same clarity. No action accompanied the words. The United States refused to act the mediator; and it was unwilling to apply to Japan the provisions of the Neutrality Act that might have cut off essential supplies of oil and iron. A conference with the powers that had promised to respect the territorial integrity of China came to nothing. Somehow it proved difficult in 1937, and in the next four years, to place a genuine obstacle in the way of the Japanese advance. That was continued at an uneven and paradoxical pace, with all our sympathy going to

Chiang Kai-shek, but a good part of our aid in 1938 and 1939 to the invaders of his country.

This perplexing policy, the President had been convinced, was necessary. Otherwise the Japanese might be goaded to still more extreme action and the hope of peace irreparably lost. For the subjects of the Mikado were themselves divided. On the one side were the Emperor himself and his intimate advisers, along with important business interests and the navy, all disposed to be reasonable and friendly to the United States. Could they but retain control, then a tolerable compromise might be evolved.

The threat was from their opponents, centering in the army. These hotheaded extremists had run away with policy in the Manchurian incident, and they were not to be offended lest they throw off the restraining influence of the moderates and plunge Asia and the world into full-scale war. In the middle of 1939, indeed, they were engaged in covert discussions with the Germans. General Oshima, the ambassador in Berlin and a deep admirer of the Nazis, hoped to turn the Anti-Comintern Agreement of 1936 into a full-scale military alliance. He was not finding this as easy as he had hoped; but the United States would be unwise, by any openly hostile act, to increase the difficulties of its friends in Japan.

In the late summer of 1939 came the first of several abrupt turns in the situation, initiated by that original diplomat, Adolf Hitler. Hitler's originality consisted of two elements: his own capacity for outrageous treachery, and the touching faith he stirred in hard-headed realists who continued to believe they could see through his motives. The fixed point in German-Japanese relations had been mutual hostility to the Soviet Union. In August, while Oshima still innocently toiled to draft the terms of the anti-Russian alliance, the Nazi-Soviet pact was being signed and sealed. For the Japanese as for the rest of the world its publication was a bombshell; and that, together with the outbreak of European war in September, called for a complete reconsideration of policy.

At the end of 1941, after the shock of Pearl Harbor, those who guided American foreign policy could hardly remember the unrestrained optimism with which they had viewed the world only two years earlier.

In 1939 the Japanese were bogged down in indecisive war in China. On their flank the Russians, released from fear of war in the West, were an imminent threat. And the United States could at any time bring the Nipponese to their knees by cutting off vital supplies of oil and iron. It was better of course not to do so at once; excessive pressure might force the moderates out of office and open the way to some act of desperation by the army extremists. In any case it was better to wait until the European war was settled. The French and British were impregnable in their fixed positions and economic pressure would shortly bring down the flimsy structure of

Hitler's economy. So ran the American theory as 1939 drew to a close.

Differences of opinion were minor and related to the rate at which pressure should begin to be asserted. There was a genuine need for stockpiling strategic materials at home and that might have been the occasion for banning exports. The President was tempted, but the State Department was reluctant. From Tokyo Ambassador Grew warned that if oil were cut off, Japan might send her fleet south to strike at the Dutch East Indies. F.D.R. replied, "Then we could easily intercept her fleet." But no curtailment of supplies was yet imposed, as it might have been under the neutrality laws and as it had been earlier in the case of Spain.

It seemed better to hold the weapon poised but not to strike. There were friends of the United States in each of the several Japanese cabinets that held office down to 1941. These elements were to be strengthened while Ambassador Grew labored to secure some sort of understanding. If no permanent treaty could be negotiated, a temporary *modus vivendi* would do until the defeat of the Germans would end American anxieties in the West.

Again Hitler seized the initiative and altered a situation he would not allow to remain stable. While Britain and France were confidently discussing the idea of sending an expeditionary force to aid Finland against

Russia, the Germans were drawing up the plans that made all Western Europe theirs. In the spring and early summer of 1940 Holland fell, then Norway and France.

The reverberations of these events in the Far East stirred the Nipponese. The difficulties upon which Britain, France, and the Netherlands had fallen could not fail to weaken their great Asian colonial empires. The fate of these possessions was of the utmost importance to Japan. Here were the rice and oil and rubber and tin its industry needed; here was the living space its growing population demanded. Expansionist sentiment flared up. The army restudied its position, began to plan for a movement to the south, and called for changes in the cabinet that would bring into being a government alive to the potentialities of the moment.

The Emperor and the circle of elder statesmen who were his immediate advisers were troubled. They had no heart for the wild adventurousness of the army cliques, and they were reluctant to break once and for all with the United States. Yet they could not but be impressed by the German achievement. What indeed if the day of the democracies were really over! Could they afford to pass by the opportunity destiny held out to them? Cautiously they moved toward the aggressive policy demanded by the army, yet with a bridge still standing for a retreat were that necessary.

In July, 1940, Prince Konoye was called upon to form a new cabinet. Some fifty years old at the time, the

Prince had had considerable experience in the affairs of state. More important, he stood above parties and factions and by virtue of his family connections enjoyed a prestige matched by few of his contemporaries. He took office reluctantly, fully aware of the difficulties ahead and swayed by the argument that only he could prevent a full swing to the extremist army position.

As it was, the army group made a critical gain. In the new cabinet, for the first time in many years, it had a friend in the foreign office. The new minister, Matsuoka, was bitterly anti-American and anti-British. It was he who had led the Japanese out of the League of Nations in protest over the resolution of censure on the Manchurian incident. He had neither forgotten nor forgiven those he held responsible for the insult. To the ambitions generated by his aggressive instincts he added the bitterness of the desire for revenge.

Konoye's influence kept the conversations with Grew alive; a flickering hope for peace or a truce persisted through the next year. But Matsuoka's energies were devoted to the diplomatic preparation for war that would make possible unlimited Japanese expansion. Three areas were of utmost importance, Burma, Indo-China, and the East Indies. In each the Japanese army had an immediate interest: in Burma, to close the road by which supplies continued to reach the Chinese; and in Indo-China and the East Indies, to maintain the flow of rice and oil and metals essential to the industry of the home islands. In each the army had also a long-term interest, as heir presumptive to the dissolving empires of the democracies.

The means toward these objectives were direct. In China, the army deflected its drives southward, and in the Western capitals Japanese diplomats began to put pressure on Great Britain, France, and the Netherlands in their extremity. Meanwhile, Matsuoka took up the task at which General Oshima had failed earlier — negotiation of a binding military understanding that would extend the Rome-Berlin axis to Tokyo. By the end of September, 1940, the foreign minister had reached an agreement with the Germans and Italians. In the way of Japanese ambitions there now stood only the Soviet Union and the United States.

Moscow, Matsuoka assumed, would be the lesser obstacle. The Russians were, after all, still linked to Hitler by the Pact of 1939 and were not likely to object to a course which led the Japanese southward away from Siberia. Matsuoka even dreamed of extending the Axis to Moscow, with the Soviets promised Persia and India in return for their acquiescence in the conquest of southeast Asia.

It would be more difficult to deal with the United States. The enigma of American intentions gave the foreign minister his deepest concerns.

American policy had been consistently defensive. Lacking aggressive objectives anywhere, the United States had aimed only to prevent, if it could, outbreaks of international lawlessness and the creation of potential future threats to its own security. Neither goal pulled it toward positive acts; both rather called for moral pressure, for the threat of economic reprisal, and for a good deal of watchful waiting. The isolationism of the period, expressed in neutrality legislation, encouraged American statesmen to hold to these attitudes as did the conviction that all the ultimate economic assets were in our hands. We could afford to let successive incidents pass with only verbal reprimands because we were certain that when we wished we could deprive the aggressors of the essential materials of their war machines and thus bring them quickly to heel.

The fall of France hardly disturbed the apparent logic of this attitude. Indeed, the loss of a continental base from which the Allies might mount a counteroffensive confirmed the defensive stance of American policy. In the dark days of the Battle of Britain when Nazi power reigned unopposed in Europe, the only basis of hope was the faith that somehow, if American supplies enabled the English to hold on long enough, the German empire would begin to collapse from within. The same faith applied to the Chinese struggle against their Japanese invaders.

Nineteen-forty was also an election year; and the pressures of the presidential campaign froze all American statesmen in their attitude of the moment. The necessity of explaining policy to the electorate led the

President to the use of terms that would thereafter deprive him of considerable freedom of action.

F.D.R. had made the decision to run for the third term in the midst of the crisis in Western Europe, convinced that only thus could he keep the foreign policy of the United States in the hands of men alive to its responsibilities as a world power. He labored through the campaign under the same conviction. He had to make the people understand the logic and the necessity of the defensive position which would both win the war and yet call for no adventures in remote corners of the earth. Twice in widely attended speeches he emphasized that "the purpose of our defense is defense" and that we would not send forces "to fight in foreign lands outside the Americas, except in case of attack." Reread a year later, those phrases would have a portentous meaning.

Read by the Japanese expansionists in the late fall of 1940, these statements tended to neutralize the effects of the first attempts to apply economic sanctions. In July the United States had ordered the licensing of the export of all scrap iron and oil, and in September an embargo was placed on the export of scrap on the same day that China was granted a substantial loan. None of these measures as yet inconvenienced the Nipponese, who continued through the winter to push their plans for the conquest of southeast Asia.

The chief deterrent for the moment was uncertainty about the intentions of their good friend Adolf Hitler.

In November, 1940, the Führer had intimated that it would not be such a good idea to bring the Soviet Union in as a fourth partner in the Axis. Not certain in the months that followed whether to regard Russia as a future friend or enemy, Matsuoka finally made flying trips to Berlin and Moscow in the spring of 1941. The Germans having been thoughtfully reassuring, he now concluded a Neutrality Pact with the Soviets; and the Japanese army prepared to put its southward drive into high gear.

There was not a little discomfiture in the Japanese foreign office on June 22 when the news arrived that the Germans had declared war on Russia. The army wished to hold to its course, convinced that expansion southward was most desirable and that the Wehrmacht would in any case quickly crush the Red Forces. Japan could then take what it wished in the north at its leisure.

German treachery, however, gave the moderates in the cabinet their last chance to press for an understanding with the United States. Prince Konoye gently edged Matsuoka out of the cabinet and began to explore the means of achieving a compromise.

Since March Admiral Nomura, special envoy to Washington, had been engaged in a series of discussions with Secretary of State Hull. Ultimately in the next nine months the two men were to hold fully fifty conferences. Nomura, a stolid, rather straightforward naval officer, had unwillingly accepted an assignment he feared would fail. He had no heart for deception and was unhappy at the knowledge that while he talked peace, his country's army actively planned war.

Hull was unhappy too. As the polite conversations moved endlessly onward, he found it difficult to maintain the requisite air of bland ingenuousness. The Americans had by then broken the Japanese secret codes, and "magic" brought the Secretary of State transcriptions of the envoys' instructions as well as full accounts of the crucial decisions of the Nipponese government in Tokyo. The niceties of diplomacy nevertheless required that he pretend to an ignorance he did not enjoy, and that comic element added to the basic futility of the negotiations.

Now in the summer, Konoye proposed a direct meeting with President Roosevelt. The face-to-face talks between the heads of states, he hoped, might uncover some level of agreement on which a compromise might be worked out. Of his personal sincerity there was no doubt, and Ambassador Grew was inclined to clutch at this straw of hope as the final opportunity to keep the peace.

In Washington, however, the plea for such a meeting was not heeded. This seemed but a tactic of distraction, under cover of which the Japanese army would proceed to the further conquests which "magic" revealed they planned. The United States was now prepared to move toward a decision. It would not sacrifice China for the sake of an understanding with the Japanese, and time was becoming critical. By virtue of a miscalculation common to many, Secretary of War Stimson was convinced that the Russians would not hold out against Hitler for more than three months; and once the threat from the north was removed, the Mikado's army would be less tractable than ever. In August, 1941, Konoye's suggestion was evaded, and later attempts to revive it were definitely rejected.

Not that the United States even then contemplated the aggressive use of armed force to compel the Japanese to withdraw from China or to head them off from other expansionist adventures in southeast Asia. The election pledges of the preceding fall certainly stood in the way. More important, American diplomacy remained fixed in the defensive posture of the past few years. It would not abandon Chiang. But it would rely in the first instance on economic sanctions and strike back with arms only if attacked.

The time had come, however, to resort to the economic weapons which many believed would whittle away the striking power of Japan. In the early summer of 1941 Britain and the United States had agreed to apply such sanctions should an attack be launched on Indo-China. On July 25, the day after the Nipponese aggression, the Americans froze their credits. This was the first turn of the vise that was to crush the empire of the Rising Sun. (The earlier embargo on scrap iron exports had been explained away as a stockpiling emergency.)

Unfortunately the Japanese Army would not keep its head supinely in position. Its spokesman now was General Tojo, a minister of war and almost a caricature of the American conception of the militarist. Personally cruel and unscrupulous, he embodied all of the army's traditional will toward power. He was impatient of the temporizing of the civilians, knew the United States was his enemy, and was not at all inclined to accept slow strangulation by talk and embargo. His own plans had already been formed in the beginning of July, 1941. Confident that the Russians would be helpless before the Germans and that there was therefore no danger from Siberia, his troops would move south to the rich prizes of southeast Asia.

All the time that Konoye strove to keep negotiations alive, the Japanese Army refused to accept the least limitation, within the cabinet, on its own freedom of action. Tojo opposed the prime minister's scheme for direct conversations with the President of the United States, and insisted that the issue be forced. When the scheme fell through, the army high command redoubled its insistence; a dramatic warning of its seriousness came in the attempt to assassinate Prince Konoye on September 18.

So far the Japanese Navy had held back; its objectives differed from those of the army, and traditionally it had been friendly toward Britain and the United States. Now, in early October, it came around to Tojo's point of view. There seemed no alternative, no acceptable way to peace; economic sanctions affected it directly and vitally; and it feared it would be completely overshadowed if the initiative passed entirely to the army.

The navy shift was the deathblow of the moderates. On October 15 Konoye resigned and Tojo became prime minister — a clear foreshadowing of the events to come. Through the next six weeks the pretense of continued negotiation was diplomatically maintained; Nomura continued patiently to call upon Hull in Washington.

But in Tokyo the decision for war had already been made.

On November 10 a Japanese striking force was ordered to assemble in the Kuriles, prepared to launch a blow by sea at a predetermined target. On the twenty-second the task force was ordered to set sail in four days and to be in position to attack on December 8. On November 27 warnings of approaching war were dispatched to Japanese diplomats overseas. Three days later word was passed to the German allies. On December 1 the imperial conference was told, and on December 6 the Emperor, and Admiral Nomura in Washington.

"Magic" had kept the Americans fully informed. Every step the Japanese took was at once known in Washington, except the precise destination of the task force that set sail at the end of November. On the twenty-fifth of that month the Secretaries of State,

War, and Navy had met with the chiefs of the forces, and the President and had carefully reviewed the situation in the light of all the facts. A day later came the final American note to the Japanese with a statement of the minimal terms essential to peace, terms the United States knew Tojo had already determined to reject. On December 6 the President read the "magic" copy of the dispatch to Nomura and concluded, in full knowledge of what it meant, "This means war."

The war, of course, would come through action by the aggressor. The United States, people and government, were thoroughly committed now to war as defense only. It was altogether inconceivable that hostilities should be initiated by the Americans; the first blow would no doubt be struck by the enemy.

Of one thing, however, the President could be sure that night. There would be no surprise. The intentions of the Japanese government were completely known, and the responsible heads of the armed forces had been thoroughly alerted. The American public and Congress had been kept in the dark, but that was necessary to protect the invaluable weapon of "magic," which was useful only so long as the Japanese did not know of its existence. But those who guided the military strength of the nation had been warned and could be counted upon to be vigilant in its defense wherever necessary.

Yet a surprise there was, and one with consequences so momentous it seemed scarcely credible later that it could have come about except as the result of deliberate conspiracy.

The United States Navy had been thoroughly forewarned. Back in March Admiral Stark had given notice to his fleet commanders that the question of American entry into the war was one of *"When* and not *whether."* For months the naval command had known what the shape of coming events would be.

Nor was it difficult to guess that hostilities would begin with a surprise attack. Every textbook offered numerous instances of such blows at a sitting fleet bottled up in its own harbor. The Japanese themselves had obliterated Russian sea power in Port Arthur in 1904; a hundred years earlier Nelson had wiped out the French and Danish concentration in Copenhagen; and more recently the British had broken the back of Italian naval strength at Taranto. These were commonplaces of naval knowledge. Less than a year before the bombs rained down on Hawaii, the Secretary of the Navy had noted that it was "easily possible that the hostilities would be initiated by a surprise attack . . . at Pearl Harbor."

Yet that possibility was never taken seriously. "Without exception," the Roberts Report pointed out, all the officers in charge of the base believed that the chance of such a raid was "practically nil." Alert #1, in effect at the time, called for readiness "with no threat from without" and the attack when it came was "a complete surprise to each of them."

Preparations for defense at the base were therefore somewhat perfunctory. Patrols were ineffective; neither the army inshore nor the navy offshore aerial reconnaissance was in operation. The harbor was unguarded against submarines; a venturesome Japanese craft was already inside by the time of the *Ward's* eventful encounter with another.

These exhibitions of carelessness sprang from the certainty that Pearl Harbor was impregnable. In the warnings from the Chief of Naval Operations to Admiral Kimmel and from the Chief of Staff of the Army to General Short, the possibilities of attack upon Guam, the Philippines, Thailand, Borneo, or Malaya were seriously mentioned, on Hawaii never. After all, Captain W. D. Puleston, in the authoritative *Armed Forces of the Pacific* (1941), had already demonstrated that "the greatest danger from Japan, a surprise attack on the unguarded Pacific Fleet" had already been averted. The fleet was "at one of the strongest bases in the world — Pearl Harbor — practically on a war footing and under a war regime. There will be no American Port Arthur."

This certainty sprang from commitment to a theory of the nature of naval warfare. Since Theodore Roosevelt's days, Admiral Mahan's ideas had steadily gained adherents and become almost official doctrine; they constituted, Secretary Knox said in 1941, "a naval 'bible.'" They created the mood that dominated Pearl Harbor in the early morning of December 7 of that year.

Sea power, the determining military factor, depended, Mahan taught, upon the creation of a battle fleet able to wipe out any combination of enemies in a pitched engagement. An effective fleet must be more heavily gunned and more heavily armored than its opponents; it must fight as a unit to bring maximum power to bear on any given point; and it must seize and hold the initiative. The battle fleet that thus controlled the sea would dominate every route of trade and determine what troops could be carried and where.

The heart of the fleet thus conceived, the capital ship, was the battleship which across the decades had grown up larger and larger from pre-dreadnought to dreadnought to super-dreadnought. All else was auxiliary: destroyers, cruisers, submarines and the rest, useful only to the extent that they supplied scouting or defensive assistance to the battleship.

This fleet existed in 1941. For its sake the United States neglected to build escort craft or submarines. It sacrificed speed to big guns, and it overlooked the value of the aircraft carriers which from the Coral Sea onward were to bear the brunt of actual attack. On December 7, the Pacific Fleet had less than half the carrier strength of Japan. But it was unmatched in the power of its battleships — all but one of which were safely stored in Pearl Harbor.

There was a design to their being there. British pleas that some of the ships be stationed at Singapore were regretfully rejected. The fleet had to stay where it was, intact, to carry through the plan of operations thoughtfully worked out from years of watching the potential Japanese enemy.

To seize the strategic initiative was imperative. Otherwise the Nipponese, from bases flanking the route to the West, could harry American fleet movements, and avoid a decisive engagement until numerous local actions had sapped the strength of the larger navy. By taking the offensive, on the other hand, the American fleet could remain intact, seek out the enemy in his own territory, carry the battle to him with superior force, and annihilate him in a pitched engagement.

The consecutive steps in the execution of the plan were clear. The available fleet would assemble in Pearl Harbor, then move to its Philippine bases, where the Asiatic squadrons would join it, then establish a blockade of the Japanese islands, and finally force a major battle.

Here was the tragic gap between naval theory and diplomatic policy. According to the theory, the imminence of war should have converted the forces in Pearl Harbor into an operative fleet, actually at sea and prepared to fight. The Dutch in the East Indies were under way by November 30, and certainly the Americans had fully as much warning.

The fleet stayed at its base because, theory or no, it could not take the strategic offensive. The exigencies of diplomacy and the state of public opinion had for years dictated a defensive attitude and continued to do so. On November 27 General Short had been explicitly warned not to move before the enemy did; and two days later Admiral Kimmel was similarly cautioned to take no offensive action until after an overt act by the Japanese. There was no question but that the first blow would be struck by the enemy; and only after that blow, or after a formal declaration of war by Congress, could the American Navy move to the offensive.

Since there was no co-ordination between diplomacy, which was entirely defensive, and naval policy, which was offensive in its presuppositions, the act of war required a period of transition from the one position to the other. The airplane made the necessary interval of time — no matter how brief — disastrous.

For the Japanese, the problem did not exist. Once Tojo was in power, military action and diplomacy were the twin arms of a single totalitarian policy directed at the same objective although using different means as the occasion demanded. The decision for war once made, every energy and any means could be devoted to its successful prosecution.

Although the army was by now in complete command of the Empire, Tojo recognized that control of the ocean routes to southeast Asia would have a decisive effect upon the outcome of the whole struggle.

Unless these areas were promptly and securely linked to the home islands, his supplies of oil and rubber and of the other commodities of war would be endangered and with them his capacity to fight. Yet there was no safety in those routes as long as the United States retained the primacy of its sea power. The prime minister knew the American fleet outgunned the Japanese even without the substantial additions in strength certain to come from the British and Dutch. That situation had to be dealt with. Realistically the army yielded the central role in the opening act of its drama to the navy.

The navy little relished the role. Themselves also readers of Mahan, the Japanese naval command, like the American, believed in the invulnerability of the greater battle fleet. They had, therefore, little faith in their own ability to survive a pitched battle. Their only chance was to destroy the American ships before the massive accumulation of power in Pearl Harbor was capable of acting like a battle fleet, and that could be done only by surprise and treachery.

The unfathomable current of events had seemed to plot for them a course almost without alternatives. They either attacked and crushed the American fleet in Hawaii, or they were lost. The expedition was formed not in a spirit of confidence but in the desperate recognition that the task had to be done. Whatever poor hope for success it had came from the knowledge that there was a gap in American strategic policy.

Perhaps the fleet would remain in the harbor until after the declaration of war, and it might be that on a quiet Sunday morning the bombers could get through!

That was a slim foundation for the great risk involved. The task force assembled at the Kuriles and made its way southward in an atmosphere of grim, almost suicidal, determination. There was little optimism among the young men who stood before the bombers on the carrier decks and prepared for the reckless enterprise before them. There would have been none at all had they suspected that "magic" had already made their deceit known to the American government.

On the day of deep tragedy for the United States, the Japanese did get through. All the opportunities for their detection failed to produce a warning that was heeded. The attack came, a complete surprise, and was thoroughly effective. It determined the character of the long war it precipitated, and it was to influence the nature of the unsteady peace that followed.

Yet it had come perilously close to failure, for even partial effectiveness would have been a kind of failure. No conspiracy kept Lieutenant Commander Outerbridge's message from being more closely studied or prevented the radar signal from being heeded. It might well have been otherwise, with other consequences. The chance that had so often played a part in the American past had done so again.

CHAPTER NINE

Views of the Past

THE sudden storm, the chance encounter, the unexpected recognition of love and hatred, supply
the elements of drama to daily life. They are also part
of the stuff of history.

Such occurrences are accidental, yet not outside the
laws of nature. That a wind should rise or a harbor
freeze, a gun explode or a man fall in love is entirely
explicable; the causes of such incidents can be understood by study of the principles of meteorology or ordnance or psychology.

But the incident is not consequential in itself. That a
storm should blow across a Virginia stream or a Dutch
port become ice-locked, that a ship's gun should explode or a Spanish maiden beguile a lonely wanderer,
these are events that would in themselves not attract
the historian's attention. Their significance arises from
their particular context. The storm rose at the moment
when an army began to escape, the harbor froze as a
fleet prepared to sail, the gun exploded with a Secretary
of State beside it, and the maiden's graces attracted a
man in process of creating an empire.

In looking backward over the past, we do not wish to admit that we are ourselves the products of a series of accidents; we grope for some meaningful connection between the incidents that constituted the turning points and their surrounding circumstances. Yet the causes of the former are independent of the causes of the latter. The atmospheric conditions that brought on the storm and the military conditions that caused Cornwallis's army to retreat were the products of altogether separate chains of causes and effects. Was then their fateful convergence simply a contingency, unforeseeable and without meaning except in its results?

The question would not have troubled historians of the seventeenth century and earlier, in America or elsewhere. In their universe a divine Providence interceded directly in the affairs of men. Marvelous occurrences were the favorite material of chroniclers and needed no explanation, for they revealed the workings of the hand of God.

From the eighteenth century onward, however, we would not have it so. We have excluded accident and caprice from our view of the past and insist that human development is the orderly product of forces working implacably over long periods of time. Our total understanding of man in his society is set within that view of the past. Yet within it where is the place for the turning points that have studded our history?

To answer, we must first examine that view of the

past and how it came to be held. We may then attempt to assess the meaning of the turning point within it.

In the eighteenth century the past began to seem less like a discontinuous series of divinely-inspired or satanically-willed incidents and more like an unbroken sequence of steps toward the present. The new conception emerged with growing clarity in the consciousness of Americans, influenced by the general historicism of the era on this side of the Atlantic as in Europe. As the universe fell into a natural Newtonian order, it was a matter of course to regard the present as the product of a chain of antecedent events, each link of which was worthy, not merely of curious attention, but of serious study and understanding.

In the United States the triumph of the Revolution and the romantic nationalism of the nineteenth century magnified the importance of the past. The citizens of the new Republic were anxious through a knowledge of their own antecedents to establish their identity as a nation. If history was, or appeared to be, increasingly serviceable also as a tool of analysis in theology and in social science, that simply added practical weight to interests already lively. The reading public turned in eagerness to the works of Parkman and Bancroft and a host of lesser interpreters.

By the last quarter of the century concern with comprehension of the past was evident in the widespread popularity of historical writing, in the flourishing societies dedicated to its study, and in its prominent place in education. Americans displayed that concern most strikingly in connection with the succession of great centennial celebrations between 1876 and 1904 which offered them the opportunity for recollection.

The publications and the orations these festivities touched off expressed what amounted to an official creed which evoked universal public assent. These commemorations indicated that Americans had by then clearly established a meaning, directly relevant to their own situation, for all that had gone before in their history.

The past, by 1875, had acquired the attributes of continuity and regularity. It proceeded in a chain of natural causes and effects, not subject to interruption or caprice. Any given moment in time was inextricably linked to all that had gone before, and each day was the product of its antecedents. Bancroft still found God "visible in History," but his Deity acted through the steady unfolding of a plan rather than through unpredictable interruptions of the natural order.

The plan was progress. Americans confidently believed that history was the record of man's improvement which would continue indefinitely into the future. From this belief there followed necessarily a negative judgment of the past which was invariably inferior to the present. Adjectives that connoted age had a clearly unfavorable implication. By contrast, terms of novelty and youth were in themselves favorable; and what was progressive was self-evidently desirable.

Yet the past was not wholly a record of error and ignorance. It was also the future in process and contained within it the origins of what was to come. It was possible, looking backward, to observe great achievements, landmarks in the path of human progress. Now and then men and institutions had torn themselves out of their context and had thrust themselves forward toward the present. Gutenberg, Luther, Columbus and Washington, Magna Carta and the American Constitution were, in that sense, in advance of their time. The men and the institutions of the present had, therefore, a particular affinity to those of their antecedents who thus narrowed the gap between past and future. Many Americans, for instance, found it possible to recognize as their ancestors Elizabethan Englishmen but not those of the fifteenth century, for Protestantism was counted one such forward-looking achievement in the history of human progress.

Looking backward at such events, Americans could make out another significant aspect of the past. For the past itself justified the changes of the present. Revolutionary change was inherent in the processes of progress, and the heroic incidents of the past related to those processes themselves confirmed the validity of further changes. Although, therefore, the past in general was inferior to the present, those features of what had gone before that were related to change were worthy of admiration and emulation.

Americans considered the incidence of such exceptional individuals and events particularly high in their own past. Their whole history was exceptional. It was the virtue of the New World to have been ever new, to have stood always in advance of the rest of the globe. American history, as the idealistic historians from Bancroft to Rhodes described it, was inherently progressive. It put into proper perspective the great transformations that Americans of the day hoped to see in their own society. By the same token the virtue of the founding fathers was in part responsible for the excellence of their descendants.

But the American past was not the exclusive heritage of those descendants. Precisely because of its mission of universal enlightenment, what had happened in the United States was relevant to the future history of all the peoples of the world. In 1900 it still made sense to proclaim, as Paine once had, that the cause of America was the cause of all mankind.

The multitudes who had actually migrated to the New World certainly had a stake in its past. It was true that the bulk of American immigrants were peasants, with a pessimistic view of life that was alien to the very idea of progress. It was true that almost all the newcomers lacked any historical consciousness whatsoever. Peasant memories rarely ran back beyond the recollections of living man; and even such people as the Jews, who were aware of a distinctive ethnic past, had no sense of chronology or of orderly historical development. The past the immigrants had left behind was a mélange of recent events, of mythical heroes, of poverty and oppression, and of a bygone golden age, inextricably confused. With that past they had broken in the very act of coming to the United States. Once in America, however, they immediately partook of the American past; it was for them too that independence was proclaimed, that Washington stood at Valley Forge. Even the Negroes found the American past meaningful in terms of their hopes for the future, although with more difficulty, since they suffered in a discriminatory present.

The belief that history was the record of man's progress, past to present, the belief that the great events of the past were acts of liberation, and the belief that the United States had a mission of universal import, survived beyond the last quarter of the nineteenth century. But while the notions were being proclaimed in Philadelphia and Chicago and St. Louis, subtle changes in attitude were in preparation that would give them a radically new context.

In the last decades of the nineteenth century Americans were increasingly sensitive to the obligation of subjecting their views of the past to the verification of science. Earlier writers had, of course, known the need of conscientious scrutiny of evidence. But they had generally approached the task with the faith that the truth was already known to them. The factual detail was malleable in their hands because its function was primarily that of illustrating the larger truth. It was perfectly logical from this point of view to omit or alter details in the interests of that larger truth.

The scientific historians, particularly those in the universities after 1900, enshrined the rules of evidence in a professional canon. These writers had their major assumptions too. But in their eyes the fact was absolutely intractable; in any encounter the general idea or ideal had to yield to the specific detail. Often this called for substantial revisions of the accepted version of the American past. So the academic historians rewrote the story of the American Revolution and of the Puritan settlement, and drew the portraits of the leading characters in terms much less flattering than earlier.

Such revisions undermined the confidence of some Americans in the exceptional nature of their own development. The newer historians emphasized in the American past the identical forces, often material forces, that seemed to have operated elsewhere. Mostly the scientific historians proceeded on the assumption that history was the product of general laws to which nations and individuals alike were subject; and indeed, in the effort to endow their discipline with scientific attributes, some were tempted to seek general laws of historical development either through analogy with the physical sciences or by deduction from the principles expounded in the sciences of man and of society.

The notion that physics or chemistry might supply a precise model for history was attractive but difficult to work out, although Brooks and Henry Adams persistently speculated on the possibility. Sociology was hardly more stimulating; the science of society supplied some helpful concepts, but in the United States was predominantly practical and unhistorical in orientation.

Anthropology furnished the most interesting clues toward a scientific understanding of the past. The science of man was, as a matter of course, preoccupied with theories of human development. In the early years of the twentieth century, widely read European and American anthropologists began devoting themselves to schemes for classifying the various species of man, for defining the human races. Influenced by the geneticists, they were disposed to believe that heredity was binding in the transmission of social characteristics and that racial qualities, passing from generation to generation, determined the course of human history. A good deal of effort went into the investigation of racial strains and into assessment of their historical import. The influence of anthropological ideas penetrated the writings of many historians, as long debates over the germ theory and over the Teutonic quality of American civilization testified.

The historians as a group were feeling the effects of

scientific influences now at work everywhere in American thought. Among intellectuals the conflict over evolution had just drawn to a close. Already battered by the older Biblical criticism, by the revelations of geology and astronomy, and by Darwinism, educated men had by now surrendered the literal Biblical account of creation and of human history. They had come to accept the long time span in which the earth had existed without man; they had learned to recognize that man's life on earth was well over 6000 years old; and they were no longer surprised at the suggestion of man's affinity to, or descent from, some other primate. Many had, indeed, adjusted their own faith in progress to these evolutionary concepts in the Spencerian or some other fashion.

But at the end of the nineteenth century these concepts were only just beginning to penetrate popular consciousness. The enormous esteem in which science was held, on account of its practical, pragmatically tested achievements, lent credibility to these ideas. Yet to accept them involved a painful and reluctant surrender of long-held explanations of man's place in the universe.

The response was sometimes one of complete credulity; the lost continent of Atlantis, life on Mars and in the bowels of the earth, the New Science, made as much sense to the readers of Sunday supplements and the popular magazines as the paleolithic era or the lost civilization of Minoa.

Or the response could be one of shock and indignant rejection. Henry Ford declared that history was bunk because it diminished the grandeur of the past he was coming to venerate. In the same way Bill Thompson and his followers refused categorically to accept the degradation of the heroic men and events of American history. And the Scopes trial was a confused and inchoate protest against the science which seemed to detract from the dignity of man by denigrating his past. Stubborn fundamentalism was a momentary refuge. But all the evidence was on the side of science; and the revolutionary concepts won their way into popular thought, just as the new history conquered the textbooks of the 1920's.

Whatever its particular manifestations, science had a restrictive effect upon American views of the past. By defining the past in terms of general laws, those who applied science to history reduced the role of the individual and minimized his part in the determination of events. At the same time science in the various forms of its application brought into question the idea of progress as a valid description of the historical process. Henry and Brooks Adams and others took an explicitly pessimistic position. More generally, the emphasis on the objective viewpoint and impersonality encouraged by these attitudes implicitly denied the possibility of judgments about the values of the present and the future and, therefore, destroyed the possibility of judgment about the direction of the developments of the past. Finally the belief that history was altogether the product of the operations of general laws ruled out the possibility of accident or alternative just as it minimized the importance of personal character. If not Washington, then someone like him; if not Yorktown, then some battle like it — such were the explanations to which the logic of inevitability drove historians. What happened had to happen.

Perhaps Americans, or some groups among them, acquiesced in the limited view of the past that science permitted them because they no longer enjoyed in their own experience the inner certainty of complete continuity between past and present. While the accepted creed of progress still dominated men's thoughts everywhere, incongruous ideas were, by the turn of the century, in many places juxtaposed with it.

If what happened had had to be, it was necessary to account for the undesirable features of the present. It was no longer enough to say that these were outmoded relics of the past! To some people the least desirable traits of their society were recent growths. How had these come to be?

The local-color literature of the last decades of the nineteenth century asked that question as it made popular a style of nostalgic reminiscence about the past. In novels, short stories, and poetry, a generation of writers had celebrated the peculiar characteristics of places that had once been prosperous, happy, and beautiful, but which were now fading into a gloomy decline. In its point of view this whole genre was unoptimistic. It extolled the virtues of the past and decried the evils of the present. Therefore it denied progress.

These writings were particularly the products of New England and of the Old South. It was understandable enough that Yankees should view their past darkly under the reflected shadows of the present. The Civil War had sapped the best energies of the North; its people knew they were declining in importance even at home; and the whole region steadily lost national influence. The more sensitive New Englanders felt themselves outdistanced by vigorous competitors elsewhere in the country and blamed their own loss of vitality upon changes in the demographic composition of the area. The original sturdy Puritan farming stock had given way to a degenerate foreign population, crowded into great cities and divorced by heredity and environment from the true sources of New England's strength.

In the South, the men who had passed through the harsh ordeals of the Civil War and Reconstruction also looked back nostalgically to a bygone happy era. Idealizing the society of the plantations, they were inclined to ascribe to it all the virtues of which their own lives were deficient. The chivalry, the honor, and the gracious living, so conspicuously absent in the present, they painted into their picture of the past; and like the

New Englanders, the Southerners consoled themselves
in reminiscences of a golden age.

In both regions the development of these attitudes
had characteristic consequences. There was a strong
emphasis on the necessity for maintaining the old virtues through the discipline of strict family life and
through traditional religious observances. There was
also strong pride of ancestry. Yankees and Southerners
were much concerned with the role of their forefathers
in the making of the nation. In both North and South
heredity was thus exceedingly important; marriage,
family life, access to voluntary societies, and other social activities revolved about it. In both there grew the
feeling that the nation's historical development had
proceeded desirably until some definite date when a
sudden reversal had taken place, followed by a lament-
able decline.

Strains of this thinking penetrated the literature that
the whole nation read in the early twentieth century.
So it was often novelty that was the villain — the in-
coming industrialist who disrupted the old way of life
of the New England village, or the carpetbagging merchant in the South, or the banker or railroad-builder
in the Western prairies. By contrast the primitive husbandmen, the simple fishermen, the cowboys, the
planters, were the heroes of the American drama.

These attitudes rested on two momentous assumptions. First, progress no longer was a continuous proc-

ess, but rather one that proceeded to some cut-off point; thereafter the appearance of progress was delusive and concealed a host of hidden evils. Secondly, as a practical matter, an ancestry that antedated the cut-off point was a legitimate test of social desirability, of the extent to which any one really belonged in America.

As these ideas gained currency they profoundly affected the elements of the population that could boast no such ancestry. The generous, open quality of the American view of the past had until then given immigrants and Negroes a stake in it. The shift of the terms in which the past was described to an exclusively hereditary basis posed the question as to whether such people could properly share in it; and that question obliged all those outsiders to justify their role in American history as in American life. There followed the long fruitless arguments over the nationality and religion of Columbus. Or was it actually Columbus who was the first discoverer of America, and not a Norseman or an Irishman or a Pole? There were zealous searchings of colonial records for hints of the saving presence of some forerunner of each American group. There were bitter disputes as to the identity of the Scotch-Irish and as to the role of various folk in the successive American wars.

Behind all this searching of the past was the eagerness to find a place in advance of the cut-off point, to establish oneself in the United States before the abrupt change that altered its history. The quest emphasized more than ever the importance of the turning point, and it suggests the utility of further inquiry into the nature of the concept itself.

It will not be fruitful to pass judgment on the particular dates men selected. Henry Adams went back to the thirteenth century for his decisive change. His more perspicacious brother, Charles Francis, writing about Quincy, fixed on 1825, when the railroad appeared. Others of their contemporaries hit on the Civil War. But the year selected is less important that the fact that so many of these people were making a selection.

They were doing so because in these fitful decades Americans had frequently had the opportunity to wonder whether human history was not open to such abrupt turnings. The depressions of 1893 and 1907 had each evoked widespread fears that all American history to that point had come to an end, and that a new era was about to begin. Strikes, from the Pullman strike to the coal strike to the steel strike, produced similar predictions. Through much of the thinking about the end of the frontier and through much of the argument about conservation ran the same frightening thoughts.

Sometimes, it was true, these speculations located the cut-off point in the future rather than in the past or present. The widespread popularity of apocalyptic literature in the opening years of the century was symptomatic. Stories about the ruin of old civilizations or about the forthcoming end of the world appeared frequently in the popular magazines and on the shelves of the booksellers. These stories occasionally took a scientific form, or they might have a didactic purpose, as in the novels of Jack London. But their central incident was a cataclysm, a violent terminus to the peaceful historical process.

Against this background, the appearance of new cyclical theories of historical development are understandable. Already Brooks Adams's *Law of Civilization and Decay* had analyzed the rise and fall of cultures in terms of a combination of economic and racial factors, to arrive at the discouraging conclusion that the disintegration of American power was approaching. Just before the First World War, the distinguished anthropologist, Madison Grant, in a widely read book called *The Passing of the Great Race,* saw in history the elaboration of primal racial forces and lamented that the American branch of the Aryan Race had already passed its zenith. Shortly after the war Spengler's dismal predictions reached the United States, and the second postwar period found Toynbee a Book-of-the-Month Club selection. None of these works influenced the writing of history. Nor were they read as history. Those who turned to them sought a foretaste of disaster rather than information about, or understanding of, any aspect of the past. The significance of the vogue of these books lay in the expression they gave to fears already current; they clothed the general dread of some apocalyptic calamity in the garb of scientific history.

In this perspective the First World War and the disasters that followed — depression, war again, and the atom bomb — were items in a familiar series. Each brought home to widening circles the possibility of some imminent turning point at which their future course would take a perilously new direction. And just as earlier the certainty of future progress had been associated in men's minds with the view of a past that embodied it, so now increasingly the fears of some menacing discontinuity in the future was associated with the view of a past that contained within it some abrupt and decisive turning point.

Alongside of the old conception of the past as continuous human progress spearheaded by the New World, there emerged in the half century after 1875 the new and contradictory attitude toward history as the product of rigid rules subject nevertheless to uncontrollable turnings. The new view did not crowd out the old. Indeed men often incongruously joined strains of both — in New Deal thinking, for instance. But the very co-existence was a change. This was a sign that some of the certainty of spirit that had animated Americans during the nineteenth century had disappeared. If there were alternative modes of regarding the past, that was an indication of uncertainty in the view of the future.

This was the significance of the insistence upon the uniqueness of the single turning point. If the inexplicable and cataclysmic could be reduced to one incident, that still left the rest of history subject to the regularity of law.

Yet what if the turning points were not unique but recurrent, breaking often and unpredictably into the paths of evolution; would that deprive the journey along those paths of all meaning and direction?

CHAPTER TEN

Turning Points

THE denial that chance played a role in history was an act of self-assurance. In the years of excited change after 1700, men who leaped eagerly at the future wished, in looking backward, to see the certain evidence of the progress with no hint of luck about it.

To limit the accidental to a unique event was also a whistling in the dark. It was a way of reaffirming that the past was regular and predictable — except for the one turning point.

In either form the unwillingness to recognize the effects of chance was a concealment of the truth.

Is it truer to speak of just eight turning points in American history?

No! Not if to do so implies that all that transpired between each of them was orderly and inevitable by the operations of some regularity or law.

For the turning points are made of such stuff as these: of a shifting wind and a courtier's slyness, of a woman's greed and an old man's hatred, of a metal's failure and a soldier's blunder. Unplanned encounters enter into the shaping of events and so too thoughtless words, the shape of a young girl's face, and the quirks of character of politicians. These are the ingredients that determine the zigzags of history; and the historian can begin to understand its course only when he perceives that it is a line made up of a succession of points, with every point a turning point.

That much is the beginning of understanding. Yet in the perspective of the past the viewer also makes out the large outlines of occurrences and long developments less susceptible to the impress of the momentary event. Another kind of book could trace, in America, the evolution of ponderous institutions, almost impersonal in the extent to which they are free of the influence of individuals or of accidents; such institutions as the monogamous family, the yeoman farm, the congregational church, and the democratic republic. Along the way also can be discerned the large outcroppings of intractable developments over very long periods — industrialization, immigration, rationalism, romanticism. Such developments and the institutions associated with them are human. Yet though they are made by man, they are affected only to a slight degree by the acts of individual men.

It may be that some total estimate of a nation's past would show that the impersonal forces that create such institutions and developments set the potentialities of the historical situation; these forces mark out the broad limits within which the line from the past can be drawn.

But at any given point there is no inevitability to the direction of the turning. The way taken is determined by the momentary convergence of a myriad of factors, personal and social; and the fact of their convergence is itself often the result of some contingency, unpredictable in its occurrence. Therein is concealed much of the drama of the past.

Rightly, necessarily, the historians of the last century gave themselves over to study of the impersonal limiting forces. In so doing they learned enough to know these were not all-explanatory. More often, now, they will devote their attention to the contingent personal factors, as those are related to the institutions of society. Answers to the neglected questions posed by those relationships can add substantially to our understanding of the past.

The circumstances of our own lives at midcentury, when the world peers uncertainly at a hazardous future, demand such an understanding. It may help men to remember now that if nothing is inevitable, and chance within the limits of the situation is everywhere a possibility, then there is always scope for the assertion of man's influence. He has not been absolutely governed by historical law, but at the numerous turning points of his past has been capable of acting freely, for good or ill, upon the opportunities the situation afforded.

Acknowledgments

THE PROBLEM with which this volume is concerned has occupied my thoughts for several years. Conscious as I have been of its importance, I have nevertheless found difficulty in coming to grips with it. Perhaps it lies more appropriately in the province of the philosopher than in that of the historian.

A fruitful hint from the editor of the *Atlantic* suggested a means by which the question might be approached in a comprehensible manner, through illustrations. I am deeply grateful to Edward Weeks for that hint and for many acts of editorial helpfulness as I struggled to compose this book. I am also obligated to Charles W. Morton, Dudley H. Cloud, Emily P. Flint, and Curtis W. Cate for thoughtful attention to my problems. Richard W. Leopold was kind enough to read the work through and to give me the assistance of his learning. Mary Flug Handlin offered the unfailing aid upon which I have come to depend. And Nancy D. Hibbard prepared the manuscript with gratifying efficiency under very trying circumstances. For the opinions contained in the book, I am, of course, alone responsible.

Chapters One, Two, Three, Four, and Five appeared first as articles in the *Atlantic*. Some of the material in Chapter Nine was originally presented to a conference on American civilization sponsored by the American Council of Learned Societies in April, 1952. In another form, that material was drawn into a paper read to the Massachusetts Historical Society and published in *Diogène* (April, 1954). It has been further revised for its present purpose.

The scholars to whom the fields of diplomatic and military history are familiar will be aware of the extent of my indebtedness to the monographs which have distinguished those fields and which have eased the burdens of research for me. To set forth the extent of my obligations would result in a list far too long for these pages; readers who are interested in pursuing these topics further may consult the *Harvard Guide to American History*, Sections 117, 118, 134, 163, 167, 168, 185, 187, 194, 225, 241, 266.

O. H.

Index